D1328490

POSITIVE FAMILY DYNAMICS

Appreciative Inquiry Questions to Bring Out the Best in Families

"Over the past several years we have experimented with Appreciative Inquiry in our retreats for couples and with the families of some of those couples. We are convinced that AI is a perspective and process that will support and make richer all relationships. This book gives great entries to begin conversations. Importantly, *Positive Family Dynamics* can serve as a tool to help us learn to change the patterns we often set with members of our families, and with others significant in our lives. Developing the art of asking positive questions is a way to change the way we relate to others, to ourselves, and perhaps, even to begin a revolution in change for our world."

> — Jane Magruder Watkins and Ralph Kelly,
> *Appreciative Inquiry Unlimited. Jane is an AI consultant and*
> *Taos Institute board member. Ralph is an ordained minister and*
> *AI consultant*

"The authors of *Positive Family Dynamics* highlight through scores of examples the unlimited power of good questions to bring out the best in our family lives. This book is an invaluable resource for those searching for ideas to enliven and enrich their family conversations."

> — Dan Wulff and Sally St. George,
> *Associate Professors,*
> *Faculty of Social Work at the University of Calgary,*
> *and both are Taos Institute board members.*

"Our 'children' are now adults, and yet, we find appreciative questions remain essential for our family. They have even helped our grandchildren make a vital contribution to our family gatherings. As we learn more about their lives, and what they value, so do they learn more about us. The generation gaps are erased. We now hope the youngest generations will take this invaluable practice into their future families."

> — Mary and Ken Gergen,
> *Mary is Professor of Psychology at Penn State University,*
> *founder and board member of the Taos Institute.*
> *Ken is Professor of Psychology at Swarthmore College,*
> *founder and board member of the Taos Institute*

"Mix four great women with topics (Families and Appreciative Inquiry) on which they are true experts and about which they carry an enormous passion, and you get a fantastic book. In *Positive Family Dynamics,* Dawn, Jen, Ada Jo and Diana show what good is possible within our family relations when we open our appreciative eyes, mind and above all our appreciative heart. The unconditional positive way in which they approach the normal day-to-day, the painful and challenging and sometimes difficult situations in our families brings new, inspired hope into our family lives and as such to our societies. By touching the core of our existence, our families, they also add a new dimension to the use of Appreciative Inquiry. By their unconditional positive questions, they bring the story telling in our families to a new, touching and inspiring level. I believe this book is a must for everyone that feels a need to (re-)discover the positive power of our primary support system, our Families."

> — Joep C. de Jong,
> *Director BT Learning Solutions and*
> *Chairman of the Board of JLS International*

"Creating positive family dynamics is not about having all the answers to life for your children; it is simply knowing what kinds of positive questions to ask to create uplifting and life-giving conversations with your family members! Dawn, Jen, Ada Jo and Diana have done a superb job bringing together rich questions to ignite meaningful conversations each and every day with our family members. This book makes a wonderful addition to your family to help *bring out the best in your family!*"

> — Jackie Stavros,
> *co-author of Dynamic Relationship Associate Professor,*
> *Graduate College of Management, Lawrence Technological*
> *University*

"This book will take your family experience to new heights, as you learn to use questions to discover and appreciate what is best in those relationships. It's a wonderful read for all, and a must read for parents."

> — Jackie Kelm,
> *author of Appreciative Living:*
> *The Principles of Appreciative Inquiry in Personal Life*

"What a wonderful resource for parents wanting to bring out the best in their families! The ideas, activities and practices so clearly presented in this book provide powerful tools for helping all families become increasingly more appreciative, collaborative and effective in creating and shaping the futures they desire for themselves and their communities. As professionals who have worked intensively with families for over 40 years, we strongly recommend this book to all family members – grandparents, parents and children. We can all be empowered by the energy, understanding and hope that will be released by the practices described in this book and the outcomes that then will be generated."

> — Dr. Robert Cottor and Sharon Cottor,
> *Taos Board Member, Taos Associate and*
> *Family Therapists in private practice*

"If everyone were to practice and use the information in Positive Family Dynamics, our world would first heal and then transform. There are practical and thoughtful questions and activities in this book which I will use in our school and encourage the families I work with to use as well. Anyone who works with children or helps people navigate their relationships in an effort to improve their lives will find in this book a treasure trove of ideas and insights. I could not put the book down and found myself eager to try out the activities on my own family. Extremely comprehensive, this book covers every important aspect of families and primary relationships in a simple way that everyone can grasp and use."

> — Jenifer Fox,
> author of *Your Child's Strengths*

"*Positive Family Dynamics* is a helpful, hopeful guide to flourishing family life. It is very useful as both a resource and a workbook."

> — Marjorie Schiller , PhD
> *President, Positive Change Core*

"I just dove into the book and THIS IS FANTASTIC! How can we get this book to moms and dads at the hospital? This is like the first 'loving instruction manual' I've ever seen 'on how to raise kids'! Deep knee bend to all of you for putting this together. YES!"

> — Leslie Sekerka, Ph.D.
> *Associate Professor, Organizational Behavior Director,*
> *Ethics in Action Research and Education Center,*
> *Menlo College*

Positive Family Dynamics:

Appreciative Inquiry Questions to Bring Out the Best in Families

An Encyclopedia of Positive Questions

Dawn Cooperrider Dole
Jen Hetzel Silbert
Ada Jo Mann
Diana Whitney

To Patricia —
Here's to
great conversations!
All the best,
Ada Jo

A Taos Institute Publication
Taos Tempo Series:
Collaborative Practices for Changing Times

POSITIVE FAMILY DYNAMICS:
Appreciative Inquiry Questions to Bring Out the Best in Families
An Encyclopedia of Positive Questions

COVER DESIGN by Kris Harmat, 2008. (kharmat@roadrunner.com)
The front cover features a compilation of pictures of the authors' families and friends.

First Edition
Copyright © 2008 by Taos Institute Publications

All rights reserved. No portion of this manuscript may be reproduced by any means, electronic or mechanical including photocopying, without permission in writing from the publisher. Inquiries should be addressed to info@taosinstitute.net

Library of Congress Catalog Card Number: 2008905795

Taos Institute Publications
A Division of The Taos Institute
Chagrin Falls, Ohio

ISBN-10: 0-9712312-9-X
ISBN-13: 978-0-9712312-9-0   Printed in the USA and the UK

Taos Institute Publications

The Taos Institute is a nonprofit organization dedicated to the development of social constructionist theory and practices for the purpose of world benefit. Constructionist theory and practice locates the source of meaning, value and action in communicative relations among people. Chief importance is placed on relational process and its outcomes for the welfare of all. Taos Institute Publications offers contributions to cutting-edge theory and practice in social construction. These books are designed for scholars, practitioners, students and the openly curious. The Taos Institute's newest series is the **Taos Tempo Series: Collaborative Practices for Changing Times**. The **Focus Book Series** provides brief introductions and overviews that illuminate theories, concepts and useful practices. The **Books for Professionals Series** provides in-depth works, focusing on recent developments in theory and practice. Books in all three series are particularly relevant to social scientists and to practitioners concerned with individual, family, organizational, community and societal change.

Kenneth J. Gergen
President, Board of Directors
The Taos Institute

Taos Institute Board of Directors

Harlene Anderson
David Cooperrider
Robert Cottor
Kenneth J. Gergen
Mary Gergen
Sheila McNamee

Sally St. George
Jane Magruder Watkins
Dan Wulff
Diana Whitney, Emerita
Suresh Srivastva, Emeritus

Taos Institute Publications Editors

Harlene Anderson
Kenneth J. Gergen
Mary Gergen
Jane Seiling
Jackie Stavros

Executive Director

Dawn Dole

For information about the Taos Institute and social constructionism
visit: www.taosinstitute.net

Taos Institute Publications

Taos Tempo Series:
Collaborative Practices for Changing Times

Mapping Dialogue: Essential Tools for Social Change, (2008) by Marianne
'Mille" Bojer, Heiko Roehl, Mariane Knuth-Hollesen, Colleen Magner
*Positive Family Dynamics: Appreciative Inquiry Questions to Bring Out the Best
in Families,* (2008) by Dawn Cooperrider Dole, Jen Hetzel Silbert, Ada Jo
Mann, Diana Whitney

Focus Book Series

The Appreciative Organization, Revised Edition (2008) by Harlene Anderson,
David Cooperrider, Ken Gergen, Mary Gergen, Sheila McNamee, Jane Watkins
and Diana Whitney
Appreciative Inquiry: A Positive Approach to Building Cooperative Capacity,
(2005) By Frank Barrett and Ronald Fry
*Dynamic Relationships: Unleashing the Power of Apprecitive Inquiry in Daily
Living,* (2005) by Jacqueline Stavros and Cheri B. Torres
*Appreciative Sharing of Knowledge: Leveraging Knowledge Management for
Strategic Change,* (2004) by Tojo Thatchekery
Social Construction: Entering the Dialogue, (2004) by Kenneth J. Gergen and Mary
Gergen
Appreciative Leaders: In the Eye of the Beholder, (2001) Edited by Marge Schiller,
Bea Mah Holland, and Deanna Riley
*Experience AI: A Practitioner's Guide to Integrating Appreciative Inquiry and
Experiential Learning,* (2001) by Miriam Ricketts and Jim Willis

Books for Professionals Series

Conversational Realities Revisited: Life, Language, Body and World , (2008) by
John Shotter
Horizons in Buddhist Psychology: Practice, Research and Theory, (2006) edited
by Maurits Kwee, Kenneth J. Gergen and Fusako Koshikawa
Therapeutic Realities: Collaboration, Oppression and Relational Flow, (2005) by
Kenneth J. Gergen
SocioDynamic Counselling: A Practical Guide to Meaning Making, (2004)
by R. Vance Peavy
Experiential Exercises in Social Construction – A Fieldbook for Creating Change,
(2004) by Robert Cottor, Alan Asher, Judith Levin, Cindy Weiser
Dialogues About a New Psychology, (2004) by Jan Smedslund

For on-line ordering of books from Taos Institute Publications visit
www.taosinstitutepublications.net

For further information, call: 1-888-999-TAOS, 1-440-338-6733
Email: info@taosoinstitute.net

Table of Contents

Acknowledgements

From Dawn Cooperrider Dole

There are so many people in my life for which I am grateful. My parents, Fran and Loy, showered me with love and acceptance as they taught me to value all human life and the world around us. My brother, David, has always been my mentor, champion, and "big" brother – caring for and teaching us to live life to its fullest. My sister Debbi and brother Daryl round out the 4-D's in our family, and as the story is told, that is how the 4-D's of Appreciative Inquiry were created. The four of us learned much about giving, sharing and being a family. My husband Gary is loving, full of life, and generous. He gives of himself fully to me, our children and his students in 4th-5th grade. My children, Lauren and Kevin continue to bring joy and meaning to my life as they grow and develop into loving, caring young people ready to contribute to the world. I appreciate my extended family of 21 cousins and aunts and uncles who taught me about the larger sense of "family". I am also grateful for my Taos Institute "family" which has been a constant source of support and encouragement. I dedicate this book to all the families of which I have been a part over the years. Lastly, I thank Ada Jo, Jen and Diana for taking this journey to create a book that we hope will bring families together in appreciative ways for generations to come.

From Jen Hetzel Silbert

I am thankful to my parents, Art and Patty Hetzel, whose fun, caring, selfless ways have underlined what it means to love and cherish family above all else. To my sister, Angela Hetzel Biederman, and my sister-in-law, Lana Henningsen, thanks for the hundreds of conversations that have brought us closer and closer together. Thanks to my brother, Christopher Hetzel, who knows how to keep it fun and light. I am deeply thankful to my two daughters, Brianna and Jocelyn, who fill every new day with more wonder and joy than I could have ever imagined. To my husband and soul mate, Tony Silbert, whose positivity, hope, and encouragement has given me the freedom to live my life as I most want to live it; I love you and our beautiful daughters with all my heart. I thank my fourth grade teacher, Angela Lettiere, for encouraging me to draw, laugh, and cry my heart out (on your shoulder); you know how to make a child feel capable, heard, and loved. What a joy ride this book has been, collaborating with AJ from my IPI family, Dawn from the Taos Institute, and Diana from CPC. I am forever grateful for these inspiring women's professionalism and friendship. To the many persons who make up my circle of family and friends: thanks for being in my life and inspiring me to bring my best in all that I do.

From Ada Jo Mann

My mother, Josephine, was a master at bringing out the best in others and I am forever grateful for her appreciative life force. Even as she slipped into her Alzheimer's persona, her joyfulness prevailed and was mirrored back to her by her caregivers. Growing up, my big brother Ray set the bar for aiming high and going for it. My daughters, Abby and Alexa and their Dad, Tom, gave me the opportunity to parent co-creatively, and we continue to engage together in seeking the way forward which we most desire. My partner, Deborah, a truly positive force in my life, reminds me often that a positive approach to change begins at home. And much appreciation goes to my writing sisters, Jen, Dawn and Diana for making the work of writing this book feel like play. Finally, I would not be writing this acknowledgment or co-authoring this book had my career path not led me to David Cooperrider. I offer many thanks to Dave for his ideas and for his example of truly "being" AI.

From Diana Whitney

It is a delight to offer this book to parents and families; and to have written it with Dawn, Jen and AJ. Being a parent is the greatest joy and satisfaction of my life. Thank you to my children Brian Kaplin and Shara Kaplin for teaching me to be a great mom. Being a sister, aunt, niece, cousin and granddaughter has given me a loving identity and many opportunities to be my best. To my brothers, Louis Cocciolone and Stephan Cocciolone, thanks for the long talks that keep us and the family together. Having a brother who died young taught me to savor life in the present. To my brother Fredrick – you are in my heart. Being a daughter has given me the foundation and freedom to be who I am. Thank you to my parents, Eleanore Stratton and Louis Cocciolone. I dedicate this book to all my relations.

From the Authors

Special thanks go to Kris Harmat, our graphic artist, who created the cover for this book with loving care. Kris also did the lay-out and formatting for the book and for both we are grateful. Abundant appreciation goes to Gary Dole, Dawn's husband, who became our final editor for the book. Gary spent many hours combing through the manuscript of the book with his eagle eyes, to find the corrections and grammatical nuances that brought the book into its final form. To both Kris and Gary, thanks a million for all you did to support this project and to bring this book to fruition.

Introduction

Families matter. They play an essential role in the well being of individuals and communities. Throughout their lives parents, children, aunts, uncles and grandparents all depend on family for identity, belonging, and nurturance. Healthy families provide support to their members of all ages – from tiny infants to frail elders.

At the heart of the family is the development of healthy children. Families provide security, opportunities for experimentation and learning, encouragement and guidance to children from birth through formation and into adulthood. Children learn first through non-verbal communication, second by watching and copying parents and siblings, and third through open dialogue and debate.

Families serve as a cornerstone of society. Taoist philosophy suggests that when relationships in a family are in order, then society can also be in order. When there is an appropriate expression of authority in the family, so it will be in society. When there is respect for differences among family members, so too will there be respect for differences in society. When there is peace in the family, there can be peace in the world.

The notion of family changes with the times. Noted family therapist, Salvador Minuchin states, "The family has always undergone changes that parallel society's changes. It has taken over or given up the functions of protecting and socializing its members in response to the culture's needs."[1] The twenty-first century ushered in a wide range of demands leading to great diversity in definitions and practices of family.

Never in history has family meant so many different things to different people. For many, a family is a heterosexual couple with two children and a dog. For others, family is the tiospya, the extended grouping of relatives within the tribe. For still others it is a single mom and three kids, or a gay couple who have an adopted child, or a lesbian couple with children from one's prior marriage, or a two career couple without children, or three generations living in the same household, or people of different faiths, races or ethnicities bridging differences and raising children in multiple languages. In this book we define "family" as all-inclusive, embracing all permutations and creations of family life.

Characteristics of Thriving Families

We've all seen families where members are chatting and laughing as they share a day or an experience together. We have also seen families where members are yelling at one another, being critical and even abusive to one another. What is the difference? What makes a thriving family? We believe that thriving families care about the quality of relationships among family members and the self-esteem and well being of each member. No matter what the size, make-up, socio-economic status or educational level of the family, we offer the following positive family dynamics as common to all thriving families:

- *Positive communication patterns* – thriving families can be recognized by the way family members talk to and about each other. They are positive, affirming, hopeful and confident. We believe that a healthy family's ratio of positive to negative communication is at least five positive for every one negative. This 5:1 ratio means that family members give each other encouragement, affirmations and positive comments five times as often as they give each other criticism. Simply said, there is more affirmation than criticism.[2-3]

- *Unconditional positive regard* – thriving families recognize and accept differences among family members, in age, interests, styles and capacities. They understand "age appropriate" behaviors and accept all family members as people who are growing through normal and natural phases of life. When challenges arise, they are able to love the person, while not accepting a specific behavior. This requires the capacity to discover and to reinforce positive possibilities.

- *Bring out the best of each member* – recognizing differences enables thriving families to nurture the best of each member. Thriving families encourage and support each other to learn, grow and become the best they can be. Each family member has something unique to bring to life and to contribute to the family and to society. Thriving families focus on helping members recognize their gifts and apply them in making a positive contribution.

- *Boundaries based on healthy values* – thriving families provide boundaries based on healthy values and they expect family members to behave within them. Boundaries are agreements among family members that specify what actions are appropriate.

Bedtimes are a good example of a boundary. It says we value healthy children and agree that a good night's sleep contributes to good health. Other boundaries include the kind of language that is acceptable in the family. For example, a family that holds the value of respect will have no name calling or cursing as a boundary. Still other boundaries include doing homework, writing thank you letters and having everyone help clean up after dinner. Boundaries create a sense of safety and propriety in relationships. They provide a path for learning and for building trust among family members. Healthy boundaries are essential for family well being.

The key to positive family dynamics is the creation of a safe and mutually supportive environment within which family members can care for one another, can positively influence each other's learning and development, and can make a positive contribution to their community and the world at large. Many people ask us how to shift their family dynamics from negative to positive. The questions and activities in this book can help you make the shift in your family from strategies for survival – the terrible twos or terrible teenagers – to strategies for creating thriving family members of all ages – terrific twos and terrific teenagers.

The Power of Questions to
Create Positive Family Dynamics

A primary assumption of the work we do, which is called Appreciative Inquiry, is that people, personally and in families, teams and communities, move in the direction of what they ask questions about, inquire into, and study. The premise of our work is simple: *we learn, grow and develop in the areas we focus upon and ask questions about*. For example, if as parents we ask about the problems our children experience at school, we are telling our children that we value problems, and we, along with our children, become experts in problems. If on the other hand we ask our children about the most exciting or inspiring new idea they learned at school, we are telling our children that we value exciting and inspiring new ideas, and we, together, become wise and knowledgeable about new ideas.

The questions we ask within our families are fateful. They set the agenda for learning, for discussion among family members, for relational development and ultimately, for action.

TRY THIS:

Read over the two lists of questions in Table 1. Pay attention to how you feel and what you think about as you read each question. Make notes in the space provided.

Table 1
Comparison of Problem Questions to Positive Questions

PROBLEM Questions	vs.	POSITIVE Questions
Why do you blow it so often?		What subject most interests you?
Why can't you get it right even with special help?		What would you say are your 3 greatest skills, abilities or strengths?
How did you make that mess?		How did you make that work?
Who said you could do that?		What will it feel like to win?
Note to Yourself: What do you think about?		**Note to Yourself: What do you think about?**
• • •		• • •
Note to Yourself: How did these questions make you feel?		**Note to Yourself: How did these questions make you feel?**
• • •		• • •

What differences do you notice between the questions in the two lists? How can you apply what you learned to improve your family dynamics?

So What is Appreciative Inquiry?

Appreciative Inquiry is a process used by businesses, schools, religious organizations, social profit organizations, non-profit organizations, governments, and hospitals to discover and bring out the best in people. It is a strength-based, collaborative approach to leadership and change. In this book we suggest ways that it can be used as a strength-based approach to creating positive family dynamics.

In its most basic form, Appreciative Inquiry is the practice of engaging people in asking questions about what they value and want more of in their life, in their relationships, and in their work. It is the practice of using positive questions to guide discussions, learning, and interactions among people.

Appreciative Inquiry is also an invitation to see the positive potential in every person and situation, and to learn how to draw it out. At the heart of Appreciative Inquiry is the belief that every person has a positive core of goodness, strengths and abilities, waiting to be cultivated – even if they are not currently demonstrating them. Appreciative Inquiry is also based upon the ideas of social construction. Social construction is the way we create our reality through our social relationships. It is through our relationships, through dialogue, through coming to common understanding, through creating beliefs, values, and relational patterns that we create the worlds in which we live. In the family, it is through relating and understanding that we co-create our experiences.

There are many resources from which you can learn more about Appreciative Inquiry and social construction. See the last section of this book for additional readings and learning opportunities.

The purpose of this book is to introduce you to Appreciative Inquiry and its application to families. At the heart of Appreciative Inquiry is the affirmative question. This book contains **56** appreciative questions designed to increase learning, listening and positive dynamics in your family. The stories shared throughout this book were gathered from our own personal experiences as well as from colleagues and friends. We hope these stories contribute to your joy and learning as you read and use this book.

What Makes a Great Appreciative Inquiry Question?

This book is full of questions that can help you create more positive family dynamics. As you discovered in the earlier activity, not all questions are created equally. Different questions have different impacts on our thinking and our feelings. Some questions create defensiveness and close down conversation. Other questions are the keys to opening the doors of communication and sharing among family members.

You will notice five unique qualities about the questions in this book.

First, they are all *unconditionally positive* questions. In our work we have learned that positive questions create safety and openness for dialogue. When we ask people to talk about problems, weaknesses or even fears, we tend to recreate those experiences in their minds and hearts and communication closes down. When we ask people positive questions – about times when they have been at their best, or the best thing that happened in a day, or the things that keep a smile on their face – we help them recreate those positive experiences and memories and communication flows.

We realize that life is not always positive. We also know, from experience, that it can be very difficult to put aside all the problems you want to address and focus on the positive. Because to what we pay attention is what grows and becomes a lifetime habit, the practice of focusing on the positive – or on what you want more – is an essential practice for fostering healthy families and family members. This sometimes means ignoring "the problem".

When my son was very young, 5-6 years old, he stuttered when he pronounced some letters and words. As first time parents my husband and I didn't know what to do so we asked our pediatrician. His response, while hard to follow, was the best advice we could have received as young parents. He said, "It is common for very smart young boys to stutter. It seems that their language coordination does not develop as quickly as their thinking. I want you to ignore it and your son will outgrow it. It may take a year or so but he will outgrow it. If you put a lot of attention on his speech patterns at this early age, they will become his habits for life." My husband and I, and all the grandparents, did manage to ignore the awkward speech patterns and my son did outgrow them. Now in his thirties he speaks multiple languages and conducts business bilingually!

Second, questions are **open-ended.** An Appreciative Inquiry question is an invitation for another person to describe their experience or perspective. Open-ended questions create space for people to answer in their own way. Closed questions such as, "Why did you say that to your grandmother?" tend to box people in and make them feel defensive. Open-ended questions such as, "What did you enjoy most about your visit to your grandmother's this weekend?" allow people to answer in their own way, based on their own experiences. Open-ended questions stimulate open communication.

> When I ask parents, "What happens when you ask your kids 'How was school today'?" the reply is, "It was fine". Then the follow up question from the parent: "So, what did you do?", the child replies, "Nothing." The parent says, "I send you to school for seven hours and you did nothing?" I usually get a good laugh about that conversation.
>
> One thing that my husband and I created was the "good to great jar" – each day when the kids come home from school we ask, "Was it a good day or a great day?" (it is a purposeful positive question) and then ask them to tell the story that brings the good or great day to life. Sometimes we write the stories down and put them in the "good to great jar". I find that even if they really are having a bad day they can reframe it and the remembering of the day becomes a good day.
>   — Shared by Jackie Stavros

Third, many of the questions ask for **stories.** Appreciative Inquiry questions seek to uncover and draw out the stories of family members' high point experiences – those times when family members felt good about themselves, their relationships and the work they did. Good questions often start with the statement, "Tell me about a time when…" or "Describe a situation when…" and then go on to draw out the details of the story. Probes such as: who was involved and what did they do, what did you do, what about the situation was fun or energizing, what did you learn from this situation, are used to draw out the details.

Fourth, many of them ask for dreams or **images of the ideal future.** Appreciative Inquiry questions build on an understanding of the present situation and ask people to share their ideas for how it can be better. Good questions ask family members to be creative about possibilities for their future. The more vivid a person's dream for the future, the more likely they will achieve it. Henry Ford said, "Whether you think you can or you think you can't, you are right." Appreciative Inquiry questions invite people to create and describe their desired situation in words and then in actions.

Fifth, the questions ask about ***ideas and emotions.*** Some people think their way through life; others feel their way. Appreciative Inquiry questions provide opportunities for people to share both their thinking and their feelings. They ask people to relate personal experiences, ideas, opinions and feelings. In this way the questions draw out the best of everyone.

Perhaps the most important aspect of a great question is that it is asked. Don't hesitate to pose a question the next time one comes to your mind. Listen carefully to the response you get. If you hear a story filled with action and emotion, your question hit the mark. Keep practicing and in time you will experience every day as "a great question" day.

Using Positive Questions to Create Meaningful Conversations with Children

In our work, we help people in organizations and communities around the world engage with each other in meaningful conversations. We know that everyone, no matter their age, gender or race, has a meaningful contribution to make; and that being invited to share ideas, thoughts and feelings builds self confidence and relationships. When we work with hospitals, communities, and especially schools, often children are involved.

Each of us (the authors) has children and has used the practices in this book to have meaningful conversations with them; and to help them learn to have meaningful conversations with their friends, teachers and family members. From our experience, we say, give these questions a try. We believe you will be surprised in a very positive way. You can adapt the questions to your situation, your family and your children.

The positive questions in this book are intended to serve as a guide for starting a new kind of conversation. While the questions can be asked exactly "as is", we encourage you to modify the wording to suit the conversation and the people with whom you are talking. Some of the questions may seem just right for a conversation between adults. Others may seem more suited to a conversation between an adult and a teenager. Others are best with young children. All of the questions can be adapted to fit a conversation you want to have with your child of any age, your friend, your spouse, your parent, or any one else. To do this, keep the flow and basic ideas of the questions consistent with what is in this book, but use your own language. Adapt the questions to be appropriate for the age and relationship of the people with whom you are talking and wanting to get to know in a new and different way.

Each "topic" is prefaced with an introductory paragraph which is intended to be read aloud to the person with whom you want to be in conversation. However, this introduction needs to fit with the age, relationship and focus of the person with whom you will be in dialogue. You can change the "voice" of the introduction to fit your situation. You may want to create your own introduction specifically designed to fit the situation you want to explore.

Overview of this Book

This book is an encyclopedia of positive questions to guide your family through conversations that are fun, informative, sometimes difficult and perhaps even, life changing.

Chapter One introduces **12 Ways to Use Positive Questions to Bring Out the Best in Families**. We offer these as ways for you to start asking positive questions within your family. We know that over time you will discover many more creative and fun ways to use positive questions. The subsequent chapters are organized around chronological stages and issues of family life that we have found significant in the experiences of our own families.

Chapter Two – **Coupling: Co-creating our Future** focuses on questions that can guide you and your partner as you embark on a life-long relationship together. Topics such as shared values, trust, celebrating "us" and even the dream wedding are explored.

Chapter Three – **Expanding the Family** introduces questions that can help you think through the many choices along the path to parenthood. In this chapter the time of anticipating the arrival of a new baby is considered, as well as the importance of holding positive images of parenting. We also explore the experiences of having a guest in our home for extended periods of time.

In Chapter Four – **Nurturing Our Children,** the questions are written to nurture positive emotions and pro-social behaviors such as joy, spirituality and family rituals. We also explore nurturing sibling relationships, school relationships, friendships, healthy habits, and conversations with caregivers.

In Chapter Five – **Strengthening the Family Unit,** the questions highlight topics to help deepen the fabric of family life. Topics such as fun family time, family rituals, creating a peaceful home, the best of sibling relationships and exploring the wisdom of our children are included.

In Chapter Six – **Launching: Letting Go, Going Forth,** the questions are about the dynamic dance between parents and children fostering greater independence. They cover a lot of first time experiences: the first day of school, a first date, a first love. They also cover topics such as making good decisions and teen driving. These questions support the maturation process of "growing up" through conversations that tap into the positive possibilities that beckon.

In Chapter Seven – **Contributing: Being the Best for The World,** the emphasis is on conversations that can help you and your family members look beyond yourselves to offer your best to others and the world around you – your community, your school, your friends in need, and our planet.

Chapter Eight – **Tough Times: From Problem to Opportunity** contains questions to help face the tough times by shifting your focus from despair to positive possibility. By using these questions to tap into your reservoir of successful moments, you can restore confidence in yourself and your family and refocus on your preferred future.

In Chapter Nine – **Aging Gracefully,** the questions encourage the discovery of positive images of growing older, lessons from grandparents, and eldercare. We can open up dialogue about strategies for aging with dignity by exploring these questions.

The questions in Chapter Ten – **Completing: Elegant Endings** are included to help you put endings into perspective. They can help you and your family care for each other during times of loss, completion and ending. The questions range from ending the day to the loss of a beloved family pet to completing a job to separation and divorce, and making the best of our last days together.

In Chapter Eleven – we offer our **Closing Thoughts and Encouragements**. These are ideas to deepen your understanding of how to use positive questions to bring out the best of your family and encouragements to keep using them, even when it is not easy.

Finally, we offer some resources which have been helpful to us over the years as we explore bringing out the best in our families.

Chapter 1

Twelve Ways to Use Questions to Create Positive Family Dynamics

Perhaps the greatest social service that can be rendered by anybody, to the country and to mankind, is to bring up a family.

— George Bernard Shaw

The questions in this book are intended to be seeds, ideas to stimulate your curiosity and communication with other family members. They may be used in a one-on-one conversation or in a small group conversation among several family members. What follows are twelve ideas for how to use questions to bring out the best in your family and create positive family dynamics.

1. To keep the good times flowing.
One way to keep the momentum going when things are going well in the family is to talk about it. And the best way to ensure that the conversations stay focused on strengths and success is to ask positive questions. So when your son or daughter brings home a great report card, consider asking, "What was it about you that enabled you to get these good grades?" Taking time to understand "the root causes of success" reinforces the success pattern and increases the person's or family's potential for a repeat success. In addition, talking about the good times is safe and enlivening for everyone ages 2 to 92.

2. To reverse downward spirals of expression and feeling.
Life has its ups and downs. There are times in every family when one member of the family has a bad day or even a bad week. Whenever someone

in the family feels bad or has what they consider a bad experience, be sure to listen to them attentively before saying or asking anything. Listening is the most healing communication process of all. Good questions can help you be a good listener.

Focusing on the problem or upset reinforces it and establishes it as a habit. Positive questions can be useful in reversing downward spirals before they become habits. Consider the teen age girl who had done well in school and all of a sudden begins having trouble with math. Reminding her of her strengths in other areas and asking her to think about how they might help her, even with math, can go a long way to making her feel and do better. A question something like, "Let's not focus on math right now. Tell me about your favorite subject and what you do to be really good at it." After listening to the answer you might follow up with, "Now, how can you do this with math?"

3. To stimulate meaningful communication.

Meaningful questions lead to meaningful conversations. To stimulate interesting and energizing communication in your family, get in the habit of asking meaningful questions about the things you really care about. Consider the following two questions as discussion starters. One, "How was your day?" or two, "What was the most creative thing you did today?" Each of the two questions stimulates a different kind of response. Question one can be answered with one word: fine, okay, good; and the conversation is over. Question two, on the other hand, requires thoughtfulness and description – the two ingredients of meaningful communication.

Whether you are having a family dinner, taking a walk in the park, or driving to visit friends, you have an opportunity to ask a question to stimulate a meaningful conversation. And remember, kids are mimics, they will remember your questions and turn around and ask them to you or their friends. One good question can be positively contagious.

4. To bring your family history to life.

Some families make a practice of telling stories about their family history. When the stories are positive, family members gain pride and confidence about who they are and what they can contribute to society. One way to seed family stories is to ask questions about the past. Many of the questions in this book can be used to gather a family anthology, a collection of stories about people and events in the family's history. One family we know made Christmas ornaments of family events and each year hung them on the family tree. Another family celebrates family history once a month. At dinnertime, family members recall stories that they remember and that they have been told about during that month. A simple question such as, "Share a story about our family, current or past, that makes you glad to be a family member" can illicit great stories and bring your family history to life.

5. To bring out confidence in family members.

Self-confidence is not something that happens once and lasts forever. All through a person's life, events and relationships can bring out self-confidence or they can knock it off center. A great way to bring out a family member's self-confidence is to remind them specifically what it is that you appreciate and value about them. This means asking yourself the question, "What do I appreciate and value about this family member, and how can I express it to them?" You may write your answers on a card, leave them on a voice message, or share them face-to-face. We are never too old for sincere appreciation that specifically describes our unique gifts and abilities.

Another way to build self-confidence is to ask the other person questions about their unique gifts, abilities, hopes and dreams. People often have low self-confidence when they are disconnected from the self they wish to be. Asking them to share their dreams with you, and taking time to listen to them is one way to help people remember what is important to them. When you do, you will be rewarded with a smile or hug in return.

6. To learn how other families do things.

It is natural to wonder how other families handle situations similar to the ones you are facing with your partners, your children or even with their teachers. There are ways to ask questions to learn how other families do things that bring out the best in the other family and the situation. However, there are ways of doing it that reinforce problems. All too often the inquiry begins with a declaration of a problem. One mother might say to another mother, "We're having trouble with Johnny's teacher. She never has time for us. How do you manage to get regular appointments with her?" In many cases this leads to a discussion of the teacher as a problem.

A better approach would be to say, "We have noticed that you have regular appointments with your child's teacher. What do you do to get on the teacher's schedule so regularly? We would like to do the same." In this case, no one is wrong, bad or "the problem". And the focus of the discussion that follows will be where you want it – on the best way to schedule parent-teacher meetings.

7. To strengthen relationships among family members.

Families are rich networks of relationships that cross genders and generations. Each unique relationship: between mothers and daughters, fathers and sons, brothers and sisters, sisters and sisters, grandparents and grandchildren, needs attention and nurturing. Taking time to discover what others in the family care about and aspire to deepens relationships. Throughout this book you will find stories of how appreciative questions were used by family members to build better relationships.

Here are a couple of ways you might consider using appreciative questions to strengthen relationships: To create a birthday process for family members to acknowledge their relatedness. Imagine having family members tell you what they value/love most about you as a mother, sister, aunt, spouse and/or grandmother; or as a father, brother, uncle, and/or grandfather. Or perhaps next year on Valentine's Day, members of your family might send letters declaring, "What I value/love most about you as my sister, brother, parent is…." Or try using appreciative questions about relatives to stimulate constructive conversation at a teenage slumber party. The key to using appreciative questions to deepen relationships is to make them fun and age-appropriate.

Affirming the value of relatives deepens relationships, builds confidence, and celebrates roles within the family. It also contributes to a positive emotional climate that nurtures creativity and self expression.

8. To plan a family event, party or celebration.
Family events, parties and celebrations vary from family to family, generation to generation, and ethnic group to ethnic group. A great deal can be learned by asking others – in your family and in other families – about their favorite family events and celebrations. Simple questions like, "Tell me about the best family gathering you have ever attended?" will lead you to discover interesting and applicable information.

Consider planning your next family vacation by asking everyone who is going on the vacation to share stories of past favorite vacations. Be sure to let everyone tell their story at a time when everyone else can listen. After all the stories are told, make a list of the most common themes, the most creative activities, the most relaxing activities and the most fun activities. Then use that information to plan your vacation. People commit to what they help create. You can increase involvement of family members – even teenagers – in your next family vacation if you engage them from the start in its planning.

9. To honor family elders as "living treasures".
In many towns and communities around the world, elders are recognized as living treasures. They are honored and appreciated for their wisdom and life experiences. This helps them stay connected to the community, feel valued and be able to pass on their knowledge and experience to the generations that follow.

The same is true for family elders. They often enjoy telling stories of their life and the "good ole days". Appreciative questions are a great way to start the flow of story telling. Consider questions like: "What was the best part of life growing up on a farm? What did you like most about having a large family? What was the most exciting thing about going to college?" Questions can be asked to draw out the positive experiences of the family's elders and enable them to share their past with other family members.

Many families find that a book of stories about the life of an elder, or another family member, makes a cherished gift for a special occasion. They provide a list of questions to family members and ask them to respond with stories and photos. Once all the stories are collected, they, along with the photos, are organized in a book. Poems, quotes and drawings can be used to personalize the book even further. These books make great anniversary, graduation and special "big number" birthday gifts.

10. To focus teachers on the positive potential of your children.
When we teach Appreciative Inquiry to people at work, they are often excited about taking it home and trying it with their families and friends. One of the most frequent stories we hear is how people change the dialogues they have with their children's teachers using positive questions; and how the teachers' perceptions of their children change as a result.

> The parents of one young boy said they were tired of going to parent-teacher meetings and hearing all the problems their son had at school. So they went to their next meeting loaded with positive questions, "What is our son's favorite subject? Recognizing that he is not good in all subjects, what subject does he do best? What do you think leads him to do well in this subject? What have you done to help him do well in this subject? What do you see as his best social skills? What have you been doing to draw out these social skills?"

Questions like these make a difference. They not only bring out the best in students, they also bring out the best in their teachers. Positive questions are bold reminders to educators that their job is to support success, not just to report failures.

11. To help family members make decisions.
Family members of all ages turn to one another when they need help making decisions. Some people simply need a sounding board, others need help broadening their thinking, and still others need help narrowing options and making a choice. In all cases we have found that appreciative questions can be used to help family members make decisions.

Support for decision making comes in three kinds of questions:

1) ***Questions that broaden thinking*** such as: "Have you considered? What might happen if you? How does this fit into your plans for that?" Broadening questions invite family members to consider other ideas or options, and collect more information before coming to closure on a decision.

2) ***Questions that deepen self-reflection*** such as: "What feelings emerge when you consider each option? What are your long-term goals and how does this fit in? What do you imagine your life will be like if you choose this option?" Reflecting questions prompt thinking and feeling about the choices to be made. They often focus on the impact of the decision on the family member's life, now, and in the future.

3) ***Questions that call for the decision*** such as: "If you had ten points to assign to each choice how would you divide them up now and why? What are the pros and cons of each possibility? What is one small step you can take right now that feels right?" Calling for the decision with questions recognizes priorities, pros and cons and the need for action. For some people decisions are made in their minds, for others they are made in actions.

12. To create a family vision and path forward.
People of all ages want to have a say in their own lives. This is just as true at home as it is at work. Dynamic families include the ideas of all family members in creating a vision and set of values for the family. A vision is a statement or a picture, or maybe even a song that describes your ideal family. It is a description of your family when it is at its best, in reality and in your imagination. Appreciative questions can help you discover your family values in order to create the family vision.

Future oriented questions evoke stories of ideal families. They may ask about real or imagined ideals. For example, "If you woke up tomorrow and our family was exactly like you always wished it could be, what would be different? Imagine that our family got an award for the family of the year, what award would we get and why? Tell me about your dream family and how people bring out the best in others. What can we do to be an even better family?"

One way to create the vision and path forward is by drawing a picture on a large piece of paper. Another way is to have family members create and act out skits of their ideal family. After the drawings or skits have been shared, gather the family together to share common themes and make commitments to the family's future.

Using appreciative questions to bring out the best in your family requires openness to listening, learning, and adapting to one another. Most likely, each family member will answer every question differently. The gift of a dynamic family is the ability to listen to peoples' answers/stories with sincere curiosity and compassion. By being heard, family members feel cared for, affirmed and included. Healthy, dynamic families grow and develop through the continued skill of listening and the acceptance of differences.

Chapter 2

Coupling: Co-creating our Future

There are perhaps many thousands of potential patterns that might emerge when two people interact with each other at the beginning of a relationship... and the differences in relationship emerge, are created in the process of interaction.

— Alan Fogel

Families come in all shapes and sizes. For many, family means two parents, two kids, two cars in the garage and a dog. For others it means two or three generations living in the same home and caring for each other. In China, for decades families have been limited to one child. In many parts of Africa the family is the extended tribal community. To these many traditional forms of family, we add single parenting, co-parenting and same sex parenting – all viable family structures in today's ever changing world.

The starting point for the creation of many families, however, is still the coming together of two adults as a couple, deciding to make a life together. The kinds of conversations people have early on in their relationship, as they get to know one another and become a couple, sets the tone and establishes patterns of communication for the couple and later, the family.

We invite you to experiment with the questions in this chapter. They are designed to bring out the best in your relationships in early courtship, coupling, and beyond; and can help you open communication and stimulate thoughtful sharing of ideas right from the beginning of your relationship.

It was a Saturday night when my boyfriend suggested we "stay in" instead of go to the movies or to a club for dancing. "I want to interview you," he said, and I couldn't help but roll my eyes and wonder how bored I might be. We had only been dating for a few months and to put it mildly, we were "on the fence" in determining if our relationship had long-term potential.

He was an attractive, flirtatious bachelor who skillfully wooed the hearts of everyone who knew him – from business consulting clients to female acquaintances. I was an outgoing but independent twenty-something ambitiously trying to complete grad school while climbing the corporate ladder. I really liked this guy, but was not about to let something one notch above a crush risk a loss of focus, or worse – another broken heart.

He began his interview by asking me about my peak experiences in our relationship and in life in general – times when I felt most alive, happy, excited and proud. After listening to my responses, I asked him about his. We exchanged many a heartfelt memory. He then asked what I valued most about those experiences – what key aspects made them stand out for me, and I couldn't help but dive deeper in sweet nostalgia. I reflected on the importance of spending time with family and the sense of calm and peace that surrounds me whenever I'm near the ocean.

As he reflected on his "valued most" recollections, we found ourselves taken aback by how much we shared in common – that at the core of our individual *and collective happiness* were the simple pleasures that come from honoring family, being near the ocean, and nurturing a loved one's passions.

Then came the Big Bang question. "Fast-forward five years from now. Your wishes have come true and life, as you know it, is better than you could have ever imagined. What's happening?"

Feelings of elation, anticipation, and hope overcame me, and yet I couldn't help but fear a haunting sense of vulnerability. *What if I'm overexposed?* The thought of my wants and desires going public and not being reciprocated or supported terrified me. *What if I actually do see long-term potential in this relationship and he doesn't?* Lucky for me, he answered first.

He described vivid images of our getting married and sharing a home together – a place to host many a celebration with family and friends. He envisioned our children playing with our friends' children, taking vacations on the ocean, and partnering together professionally to lift up our passions in business consulting. My pulse hastened and I began to tremble, but this time from relief, not fear. I knew in that instant that he was the one – who I wanted to spend the rest of my life with, and better still – that he wanted to spend his with me.

Less than six months from that Saturday night, we broke ground on the new home we bought together. Six months after that, he proposed to me in the house as it was being built. We later married in the Bahamas, and just *ten* months after that we gave birth to our daughter which catalyzed our longing to be closer still to family and compelled us to move to the another state where we purchased a home that just happens to be five minutes from five different beaches, and to this day we count our blessings for that Saturday night interview that has helped us realize all our greatest dreams – first as a couple, now as a family.

As this story illustrates, the questions you ask of your loved ones matter. They create the agenda for your conversations and determine what you learn about each other and what you share with each other. Because of this we say, inquiry and change are simultaneous moments. As the preceding story illustrates, the act of asking positive questions while courting can plant seeds for a long and happy married life together. The more positive your questions the more positive your future together will be.

Like the couple in this story, many people who have learned about Appreciative Inquiry at work have also used it to build, enhance and celebrate their personal and intimate relationships. Many have started the habit of doing Appreciative Interviews on Valentine's Day, birthdays or anniversaries. You may want to choose a day that is special for you, a holiday or any day, and use a question from this chapter to enjoy celebrating life together, to strengthen your relationship or to help you decide how to go forward together.

Appreciating the Best of Our Relationship

The love between us as a couple is the bedrock of our relationship. It is what will hold us together during the best of times and during the inevitable rough spots that life has in store for us. What we value most about each other will help us grow and develop over the years. What we enjoy most about our relationship and time together will serve as building blocks for the future.

1. Looking at your entire experience with me – from the day we first met to now – tell me about a time when you felt most alive, most fulfilled, or most excited for us to be together. What was happening? What were we doing? What made it exciting? Who/what else was involved? What was it about me that helped make you feel so alive? Tell the story in detail so that I might relive the experience with you through your telling.

2. Let's talk about some things you value deeply – specifically, the things you value most about yourself and our relationship.

   • Without being humble, what do you value most about yourself as a person?

   • What do you value about the relationship we've created together?

   • What is the most important thing this relationship has contributed to your life?

3. Think of a time when you have experienced the things that give meaning and life to our relationship? Give some examples of how you've experienced this in action. What was happening? What stands out for you?

4. What three wishes would you make to heighten the vitality and health of our relationship?

5. Fast-forward to five years from now. Your wishes have come true and life, as you know it, is better than you could have ever imagined. From our relationship, to our lives at work, with friends, with family, and at home, we have a lot for which to be grateful. What's happening? Tell me what you see.

6. What small steps/changes can we make today that will get us closer to making this future image a reality today? Further, what support will we need, both individually and together, in order to take those steps fearlessly and joyfully?

Shared Values in Action: Getting "In Sync"

At the root of every couple's triumphs or tears is a longing for shared values – wanting to understand and feel understood, being "in sync" with what matters most to the other person, and seeing evidence of this congruence – this deep, unbreakable connection – in everyday words and actions.

1. Think back to a time when you felt fully understood by another person (family member, colleague, lover or friend) – a time when, without a doubt, you felt the other person "got it" in a manner that made you feel visible and heard. What happened? What did the other person(s) do or say that made you feel profoundly understood? What did *you* do or say that contributed to your having experienced this sense of shared values and understanding? Please tell the story.

2. Consider now the broader web of relationships that make up your network (from home, to past and present relationships at school, work, within your community, and beyond).

   • With whom are your values most closely aligned?

   • What evidence or indicators of shared values do you see in action?

   • What role or contribution are you making to support this values alignment?

   • What lessons can we draw from these relationships moving forward?

3. Now reflecting on our relationship, like all couples we have many values in common and some not. When we are at our best we act on our shared values and respect our differences.

   a. What values do you believe we hold in common?

   b. Tell me about a time when you believe we have been at our best recognizing and respecting our differences?

4. Imagine that it is several years from now and that an issue/conflict previously unresolved in our relationship has snapped sharply into focus. We're relieved and grateful to have come this far, and confident and optimistic about the path ahead of us.

   • What's been resolved? And how?

   • What steps did we take – both individually and together – to resolve the matter and heighten our awareness/consideration of each other's values?

Being Trustful and Willing to Trust

Trust is at the heart of successful relationships. A trustful relationship means that both partners are both trustworthy and willing to trust. It is one thing to deem another as "trustworthy," but it is quite another to be willing "to trust". More than giving the other person the opportunity to demonstrate his/her trustworthiness, we need to take stock of our own desire and aptitude to trust, to lower our shields of doubt brought on by yesterday's wounds and to be open to new possibilities – to be trustworthy and to trust.

1. Think of a person in your life who you trust 100% (spouse, lover, friend, family member, colleague), in whose sincerity and good intentions you have complete faith. Now tell me a story of this person and your "trust in action". What happened? What did this trust look and feel like? How did you know it was there?

2. What can we learn from this situation to become more trustworthy and to be more willing to trust in our relationship?

3. Thinking of your relationship with this person, what activities, actions, and patterns within the relationship helped to create this trusting relationship?

   - What is it about this person in relationship to you that creates this "trustworthiness"?
   - What is it about *you* that made you willing to trust? Be specific, and aware of those attributes within you that make your ability to trust so strong.

4. What *one change* can you make for yourself today – something from *within* that only you can own or control – that will improve your willingness to trust others? Share an example of that change in action. What does it look like? How do you imagine this effecting the relationship?

Deep Listening – Feeling Heard

Life comes at us fast. Sometimes the pace is so swift, conversations come and go in a blur, or worse – they get lost in translation amidst phone, email, or text messaging traffic. Other times, we get so engaged in a conversation that it feels like someone pushed the "pause button" on life – that the world stopped turning so we could, without interruption, listen deeply and be deeply listened to in return.

1. Tell me about a time when you were part of a relationship where "deep listening" occurred – a time when you felt completely heard and understood by another person. Who was involved and how did you know he/she was listening so intently? What did you and the other person do to help make this so? How did it make you feel?

2. In your opinion, what are the three main ingredients of deep listening at its best? Please describe what these look like in action.

3. Why is deep listening important?

   - What value or impact does it bring to our relationship, our lives at home, at work/school, or to the broader society?

   - What are some of the things that you think we already do that encourages and reinforces this sense of "deep listening"?

4. Finally, what ideas do you have for how we can further enhance our capacity for deep listening within relationships? And what commitments are you willing to make to further build on your ability to listen deeply?

Planning Our Dream Wedding

For many people their wedding day is among the most memorable days of their lives. For some, however, planning a wedding can be just as stressful as it can be joyful. As we begin our journey as life partners, it is important to explore each other's hopes for a "dream wedding", to stay on course with those hopes, and to plan our special day with intention – dreaming big and choice-fully.

1. Thinking back to your earliest hopes for marrying me, describe the moment when you knew I was "the one". What were we doing? How did you know? Tell me the story.

2. Let's talk for a minute about the things we value most about our young relationship.
   - What do you value most about me?
   - About yourself?
   - About our relationship?
   - How might we honor these qualities in our wedding?

3. Close your eyes and picture your dream wedding with everything just as you've always hoped it to be – your greatest aspirations realized. Please describe it in detail.
   - Where are we?
   - Who is celebrating with us? What are they saying and doing? How are we involving them?
   - How are we honoring each other, our values/beliefs, and our loved ones?

4. What steps can we take now and over the next several weeks and months that will have the greatest impact on realizing this dream wedding?

Celebrating US: An Interview with My Valentine

Shared by Christine Whitney Sanchez.

Building the life we want together sits on a foundation of commitment, is stabilized through deliberate hard work, is uplifted by fun, and is held together by the bonds of love and spirit.

You are my Valentine every day of the year. On this Valentine's Day I am reminded of why I love you. I want to ask you some questions to help us remember our good times, to celebrate us as a couple, and to inspire us to continue growing together and building our future together.

1. What are the two or three most inspiring or rewarding experiences of our time together? Please tell me a story about one of them. What was the situation? What made it rewarding for you? What did you learn about me, yourself and us at that time?

2. What first attracted you to me? (qualities, behaviors, potential)

    - What do you value most about me now?
    - How has our relationship helped or benefited you the most?
    - What challenges, disappointments or roadblocks have we successfully addressed together?
    - How did we move beyond to a new and enriching place?

3. As you think about our future together, what are your most positive hopes and dreams for us?

    - What are some of the specific things that we are good at that we can do more of to realize these hopes and dreams?
    - What do you commit to do to increase the strength and vitality of our relationship?

Chapter 3

Expanding the Family

There are only two lasting bequests we can hope to give our children. One of these is roots, the other, wings.
— Hodding Carter

Families expand and grow in many exciting – and often challenging – ways. For some, it's the arrival of a new child through pregnancy or adoption, and for others it's the welcoming of extended family, friends, and care providers into the home. For still others it is when two families join each other and create a new "blended" family.

Whatever the impetus for family growth, it is sure to stimulate the need for conversation and shared decision making. A family of two newlyweds is not the same as a family with children. How do you know if you are ready to make the change? A single parent family creates habits and ways of being together. When two single parents fall in love and decide to marry there are new relationships to be made across families and decisions about where to live, how to share space, and things as simple as who cooks, cleans and does the grocery shopping. While expanding a family is most often filled with love and deep respect for life, it is also a time for open conversation and meaningful inquiry into the best of family life.

John and Mary were ready to have a baby, and though the decision to expand their family came easily, the process of conceiving did not. They experienced several setbacks making it difficult to keep a positive outlook.

One day John asked himself: What are my greatest hopes in becoming a father – why does being a father continue to matter so greatly, in spite of the difficulties we are experiencing. His answer came in the form of a vision. He saw a little girl running toward him with arms wide open, and felt how his own heart swelled with anticipation and pride. He realized that this child didn't have to look like him or even carry his blood for him to feel the utmost care, hope, and joy for her – to feel the unconditional love of being a dad. And suddenly his desires were compellingly clear; somewhere, a little girl was being born longing for his love. Adoption was not just an option for expanding their family; it was an imperative.

Within months, John and Mary found themselves expectant parents at last. It took much patience, paperwork, interviews, and passport stamps, but they knew the reward was worth the wait when, with tears of joy, they held their daughter for the first time. Though born on Chinese soil, their daughter will forever belong to their family tree.

As this touching story tells us, when we ask a question – whether of our self or of another person – we need to be open to the surprise of the answer. The best questions are provocative and life affirming. In delicate times like the one in John and Mary's story, you can always trust appreciative questions to lead to positive, compassionate and life affirming answers – they just may not be the ones you planned to hear!

The following questions can support you in having the conversations needed to expand your family with grace, in ways that strengthen your relationships though conscious decision making and plant the seeds for a long and happy life together.

Making the Choice to be a Parent

The transition from life as a couple, or as a single person, to parenthood is loaded with excitement and anticipation, as well as fear and uncertainty over the significant changes that lay ahead. The more choice-full we are in planning our family, the more enriching our transition to parenthood is sure to be.

1. Thinking back to your earliest hopes for being a parent, describe the moment when you knew you wanted to become one. What were you (or we) doing? What feelings did you have? Tell me the story. What did parenting look/feel like to you then, and how does it look/feel like today?

2. What are the three greatest strengths that you bring to parenting?

3. What do you value most about your own parents/guardians? What do you value most about yourself as a parent-to-be?

4. What three wishes do you have for yourself as a parent-to-be?

5. Fast forward to several years from now and picture yourself hosting a family gathering, surrounded by the comforts of your closest loved ones and a delicious meal. Scanning the faces and conversations before you, you are delighted by who and what you see. You're very proud and grateful for the family you've created and nurtured – it's the family you've always dreamt of building and belonging. Please describe what you see and hear. What are the core qualities that make up *your family*?

6. What steps can you take now and during your lifetime as a parent that will have the greatest impact in realizing and nurturing your dream family?

Blissful Expectancy – Anticipating a New Addition

Whether pregnant or preparing to adopt, the anticipation of a family's new addition is filled with preparation activities and complex emotions. The following questions invite you, your partner, and family members to reflect on the high points of this experience, the life-giving forces that are key to a most blissful expectancy.

1. What key aspects of this expectancy are you the most proud and grateful, and why?

2. What special gifts or strengths do you bring to this expectancy?

3. On a scale of 1 to 10 (10 being the "Most Blissful"), how would you rate your expectancy experience thus far, and why? What does your "10" look like? Please describe in detail.

4. What commitments are you willing to make to achieve your "10" and what support and/or additional resources/guidance do you need to see this through?

New Baby, New Love: Re-defining and Celebrating Ourselves as New Parents

Welcoming our new baby into the family brings many joys and challenges, much laughter and tearful moments, times of exhaustion and times of exhilaration. From late night feedings to diaper duty, there is much work to be done and many new responsibilities to take on. As new parents we have boundless love, immense joy, big dreams, sleep deprivation and exhaustion all at the same time. Our relationship is changing as we are now fulfilling our new role as parents. It is a time to celebrate and nurture our little one, while also celebrating and nurturing each other, our relationship, and the love that first brought us together.

1. Tell me your proudest moment as a new parent – a time filled with wonder, joy, and hope for our new baby and for yourself as a new parent. What happened, what were you doing, and who was involved? What qualities about yourself stand out for you in that story?

2. Tell me about a time when you enjoyed watching me playing with or caring for our new child. What was I doing and what was our child's reaction? How did it make you feel? What specific qualities about me did you notice in that moment that you admire?

3. When as a new parent have you felt most loved, most cared for, most supported by me? When have you felt closest to me since the arrival of our new addition? Tell me the story. How has our new addition enriched our relationship with each other?

4. Share with me a time since the arrival our new baby, when we have turned a disagreement or difficult moment into an opportunity for growth, love and care? What happened and what did we do together as a couple to make the best of the situation?

5. What hopes and wishes do you have for yourself as a new parent? For me? For us as a family? For us as parents, partners, soul mates who love each other very much?

6. What steps might we take to ensure that these hopes and wishes come true?

Welcoming the New Baby: Feeling Loved

When you were born the whole family welcomed you with hugs and kisses and oodles of love. We were so happy and excited to bring you into our family. Soon you will be welcoming a new brother or sister.

1. There are many things that people can do to help another child feel loved at home. What are some of the things that Mommy, Daddy and other family members or siblings do now to make you feel loved?

2. Why is it important to feel loved?

3. How can you make a new baby feel loved? What other things does a baby need that you can help with?

4. What three wishes do you have for welcoming the new baby to our family?

5. What can mommy, daddy, and other family members or siblings do more of to make you feel loved and supported all the time at home?

6. How can you and your siblings make your mommy and daddy feel loved and supported in return?

7. What new roles/tasks might you and your siblings take on to show your parents that you love and support them in welcoming the new baby to our home?

A Sense of Belonging

When we open the door of our home to extended family (or care-givers, au pair) we redefine what it means to *belong* and *be at home*. Creating this sense of belonging is a gift to both the family and the guest in the home who can become an integral part of the family.

1. Tell me about a time when you felt a strong sense of belonging – to a particular team, group, or family. What was happening? How did that make you feel? Who/what contributed to that sense of belonging? Tell me about that experience.

2. Why is it important to *belong*? Why is it important to feel *at home*? What do we all gain when there is a shared sense of belonging in our home?

3. What three wishes do you have for helping (extended family member or care giver's name) feel at home in our home? What three wishes do you think he/she has for us?

4. What's one small step *you* and *(person's name)* can take today that will get us that much closer to living out our values related to opening our home to others?

Living in Another Family's Home

There are times when we enter into another home/family. We might have the opportunity for an extended stay with relatives, neighbors, host-families, or friends. Our presence in another family can serve to bring out the best in ourselves and in our "new" family.

1. Thinking back over your life, recall a time when you became an integral part of another family. Perhaps it was when you were a child and you stayed with your best friend's family for a week while your parents went on a trip. Or perhaps it was a time when you lived with cousins or grandparents for a time. Or perhaps it was your time with a host family while studying abroad.

   Tell me about that experience. What happened that helped you feel a part of the family? How did they welcome you? What did you do to integrate yourself into the family rituals, patterns, and flow?

2. What did you value most about your experience within the "new" family? What did you value most about the way you entered this new family?

3. There may come a time when you will stay with another family/friend/relative again for a period of time. What three wishes do you have for making this experience exceptional for everyone involved?

4. What can you do and what can others do to make this experience memorable and positive for everyone?

Chapter 4

Nurturing Our Children

If a child is to keep his inborn sense of wonder, he needs the companionship of at least one adult who can share it, rediscovering with him the joy, excitement and mystery of the world we live in.

— Rachel Carson

Every appreciative or positive conversation we have with our children presents a learning opportunity. By asking the question, we take on the role of listener and learner, and the other person becomes the sharer and teacher; and we both stand to learn and grow immensely from the stories and insights revealed. We learn what it takes to get more of a good thing, how to build on past achievements, and how to imagine still greater possibilities moving forward. Best of all, we strengthen our appreciative eyes – our ability to see the good, the loving, the hopeful in ourselves and in our children. In every appreciative question, and in every positive conversation we have with our children, there is also an opportunity to develop and grow relationships. We offer the following set of questions as opportunities for you to nurture the appreciative patterns, develop an appreciative eye, and grow the relationships in your family and in you.

The soccer season had started and my 5th grade daughter had joined the soccer team again this year. The first few weeks of practice and games were moving along, however, my daughter did not have a good word to say about any of it. By the third game she was feeling as if she was not a "good" soccer player. After the game, while we were driving in the car, I asked her to tell me what she thought was the best part of the game for her. What did she feel good about related to the game? She could not think of anything at first. She told me she thought she was terrible at soccer and that she did not help her team at all. I continued to help her find one thing that she did during the game of which she could be proud. I asked, "Remember when Annie got the goal, what did you do to help make that happen?" She replied, "I received the pass from Sara, then passed the ball to Annie, then Annie made the goal." I asked her how she felt about assisting Annie with the goal. She realized that she made a great contribution to the outcome of the game. I then asked her, "What would have to happen, what would it look like, for you to have your best soccer game ever?" She immediately replied, "I would make a goal." We spent the next few minutes outlining what it would look like if she made a goal, what she would have to do, who would assist. She had a very clear image in her mind of what it would look and feel like to make a goal in a game. The next weekend she made the first goal of her life, and then went on to score two more goals. She was ecstatic and the image of herself as a soccer player increased literally by leaps and bounds. The conversation we had in the car that day was nurturing, accepting, and helped my daughter live into the success she imagined.

This story reminds us all of one of the most important qualities of a good parent – persistence in seeking success. The mother in this story didn't just ask one question. She asked a series of questions all intended to help her daughter discover her own abilities and goals as a soccer player. It paid off as the "goal" was achieved. And, not only was the child nurtured, but the relationship between the mother and daughter was strengthened.

The questions in this chapter can aid you in bringing out the best of your children, friends and family members; and nurture them on their life journey.

Nurturing JOY

Children are naturally joyful. Joy is full of love, it is a healing energy, it is a oneness with others and the universe. Peggy Jenkins, in *The Joyful Child*, writes, "Joy is the presence of love for self and for others, a state of gratitude and compassion, an awareness of being connected to our higher self and of being one with everything." Joyful children emit that unconditional love that is at the base of all joy. We can see their inner joy through their voice, their facial expressions, their energy, their excitement. How do we nurture this natural joy within each child so that throughout life, he/she continues to express, share and choose joy no matter what life challenges, problems, or struggles enter in?

1. Think back to a time in your life when you were full of joy – a joy that existed within you. Tell me about that time. Share in detail the experience. What was happening? What thoughts were going on within you? Who else was involved and what were they doing? What were you feeling about the others in the situation? What were you able to do with the joy and how did it affect you and those around you?

2. What do you value most about your own sense of joy and wonder? Where does it come from? How do you keep your joyful spirit alive?

3. As a parent, how do you encourage and support your child's joyfulness?

4. When you imagine a future for your child that is full of true joy, what do you see? To move towards this image, what can you do everyday that will encourage a sense of inner joy, strength, and love?

Best Friends Forever

A good friend is someone you cherish. Someone you like to spend time with. Someone with whom you can share something personal and know that it will be kept in confidence. Someone you care about deeply. You know when someone is a good friend because there is a deep sense of trust, care and mutual understanding. You think about that person and want to talk and share life experiences with them.

1. Think about someone who was or is a good friend to you – someone who makes you feel cared for and respected. Someone who earned your trust over time. Tell me about that relationship.

2. Now, please share with me a time or experience with this person that demonstrates the care, respect and trust within this relationship. Perhaps it was your first chance meeting, or a time of hardship when having this person's help meant a lot. Please tell me the story. What happened? Who was there? How did this person make you feel?

3. Now, recall a time when you were called upon to be a good friend to someone. What happened? How were you involved? What do you value most about yourself as a friend?

4. What would you say are the core building blocks for creating (and nurturing) an atmosphere of friendship?

5. What three wishes do you have for making your current friendships better than ever, more rewarding, energizing, and fun than you could have ever imagined?

6. What new steps do *you* feel ready to take to make those wishes a reality?

Life-Long Learning: The Joy of Learning

Children are naturally curious. They explore, experiment, and engage in learning all the time. When we create an environment for exploration, learning is a natural process. Let's discover what it takes to create the *Joy of Learning* so that it flourishes and grows in our children throughout their life.

1. Think back to a time when you were really excited about something you were learning. A time when learning came alive for you. A time when what you learned became an integral part of who you are today. Tell me about that time. What was happening? Who was involved? What did you do? What did the others do? What was it about you in that experience that brought about a profound sense of learning and growth?

2. What did you value most about that experience, yourself and the people involved?

3. We have all had at least one teacher or mentor who has inspired us to learn about something new and filled us with a love of learning. Who was your special teacher/mentor? What was it about that person that inspired you? How did they help to make learning fun and interesting?

4. Imagine now that you, as a parent, are excelling in creating strength-based and positive learning environments and opportunities for your children. Your children love learning new things when you are a part of that experience. What are you doing? What is happening that is leading to this love of learning? Tell me about it. What is happening in them? Who is involved? What are they doing? What is the outcome?

5. When you think about structured learning environments (school, church/synagogue, community settings), what can we do to create environments that encourage the type of learning you just described? Share with me at least three things that you can start doing today to help foster a joy and love of learning for the children in your life?

Parents, Teachers and Caregivers:
Partners in Bringing Out the Best in Our Children

As parents and as teachers/caregivers we are afforded numerous opportunities to acknowledge, amplify and celebrate the strengths we see in our children – to look for and elevate the many gifts and talents our children bring to the classroom, to the playground, and at home.

1. Of the many subjects my child studies in your classroom, in which does he/she perform exceptionally well? What's his/her favorite? What do you think leads him to do well in this subject? What have you done to help him bring out his best?

2. What do you notice as my child's best social skills? Please tell me a story of these skills/qualities in the classroom (or on the playground). How have you been helping to draw out these skills?

3. What wishes do you have for my child as he/she readies to advance to the next level? What can we as parents, and you, as his/her teacher, do to further support him and bring out his greatest strengths and qualities?

Healthy Habits:
Eating, Exercising, Getting the Job Done

We know that making healthy choices creates healthy habits over time. The food we eat, the kind of activity and exercise in which we engage, following through with a job or chore, cleaning up after ourselves. It is important to keep our mind, body and soul healthy. The choices we make everyday help us to stay healthy. What does it look like when we are nurturing these healthy habits in our children?

1. Tell me about a high point in your life related to healthy living, healthy habits, or a job well done. It might be a time when you experienced exceptional physical health, or a sense of well being, or organized your home in a way that you were very proud. What was it about that time in your life that led you to excel in this area? Who was involved? What was it about you that made this experience possible? How did you continue to foster the healthy living in your life?

2. Tell me about a time when you felt healthy? A time when you did something that made you feel that you were helping yourself become healthy. It could be a time when you exercised, did a fun physical activity, created a healthy meal, organized your room, or other activity. Tell me about that time. What was it? What did you do? Why did you choose to do that activity? How did it make you feel? What do you value most about that experience? What do you value most about yourself related to that time?

3. What do you value the most about your ability to keep your healthy lifestyle going at that time?

4. When you think about how you felt at that time in your life, imagine that your future is filled with healthy living habits? What does that look and feel like? How do you make it happen everyday? What encourages you to keep a healthy lifestyle?

5. Imagine now, that over the next six months you do everything you can to choose healthy habits, exercise, eating right, keeping organized. What do you see in six months time? Describe for me exactly what you are doing on a daily basis? Who is with you? What are they doing? What does it look and feel like to be living a healthy lifestyle? What keeps you going?

6. Now, let's think about three things that you can start doing today to move yourself toward that vision? What will help you keep going? How will you continue to live this vision for yourself?

Nurturing Spirituality

Our "spiritual life" is part of our journey on this earth. There is a spiritual essence in all of us which is part of our daily living and existence. We can nourish our spirituality through reflection, prayer, meditation, awareness and listening with our heart.

Nurturing spirituality involves taking time as a family to share stories of sacred times, times when we have connections to music, nature, and life. For some it is a connection to God, to others it is a connection with nature, and still to others it is a connection to the universe. Many families follow the path of a particular religion or spiritual practice. Some do not. When our lives are full of wonder, amazement, or faith, we can look at each other and the world around us with new eyes.

1. Reflect upon spirituality in your life and your experience with a spirit-filled life. Tell me about a time when you felt especially nurtured spiritually. What was the situation? What was happening? Who was involved and how did they help to nurture your sense of spirit?

2. When you feel most connected to God/Spirit/Creator/Universe/Nature, what are you doing, what is happening? What is it that leads you to feeling connected and how does this impact who you are and how you live on a daily basis?

3. What can we learn from this situation to better nurture our spiritual journey and spirituality in our family?

4. What is your greatest hope for your life related to spirituality?

5. What do you most want your children to know, experience and learn related to creating a relationship with God/Spirit/Creator/Universe/ Nature? What can you begin doing today that will help your children connect with their spiritual life?

Chapter 5

Strengthening the Family Unit

We have the power to create within our homes peacefulness and nurturance, giving ourselves and our children a base of each to take out into the world.
— Naomi Drew

Strengthening the family as a whole involves many things: making time for family conversations, showing respect to each family member, caring for each other in good times and tough times and showing how much we love and care for each other. It is a continual undertaking to see the best in each other and to affirm everyday the specialness of the others in the family. Strengthening the family unit is more than "what" the family does together; it is "how" the family does it together that creates the healthy, growing family unit.

The following story is from the book *Dynamic Relationships: Unleashing the Power of Appreciative Inquiry in Daily Living*, written by our colleagues, Jackie Stavros and Cheri Torres.

One Saturday morning the family woke up and each person had something in mind that he or she wanted to do that day. The question posed to the whole family was: What would you each like to do today? Dad: 'I'd like to go running and get some exercise today.' Adam (4 years old): 'I'd like to go on a hike and use our new hiking sticks Dad made.' Ally (6 years old): 'I'd like to pick flowers.' Mom: 'I'd like to eat a healthy breakfast and replace some of the dead greenery in our house.'

As they shared their images for a quiet Saturday morning, looking for ways to make it work for everyone, the morning activity became clear. Ally finally suggested: 'Let's eat some healthy cereal and grab our hiking sticks, and I will share mine with mom because she does not have one, and climb the hills behind the house where we can pick flowers and find mom those green things for her planters.' Their simple images and words became a fun-filled reality. They also changed the way the family related for the day, staying together and yet meeting everyone's interests.

The family in this story took the time to value each individual. They did this by listening to each person and collaborating on developing the activity for the day that included everyone's hopes for a good Saturday. They showed respect by listening to and incorporating each person's ideas. It is how we live with each other in family that creates the strong family unit we most want.

You can use the questions that follow to highlight and enhance what you already love about your family. By talking with family members about what you all really appreciate about your family you will strengthen it.

Family Fun and Rituals

How you spend time together as a family and the traditions and rituals you cherish are part of building a healthy, happy family. When you take time to collaboratively explore what is important, fun, energizing and life-giving for each person in the family, you can blend these into family time. There is an old saying that "A family that plays together, stays together." Think about it. When your family spends time doing the things that each member enjoys, then your family time becomes special, meaningful, joyful, and something to cherish. Working collaboratively to decide how to spend family time is a gift that will last a lifetime.

1. When you think about family time, what are a few of the highlights for you, times when your family spent time together enjoying each other's company? Now choose one and tell me about it in more detail. What were you doing? How did it happen that our family enjoyed that time together? How did this impact our family relationships?

2. What specifically do you value most about spending fun, quality, and enjoyable time as a family? How does this time contribute to your development as a parent, spouse, child, sibling, family? How does it contribute to the other individuals and to the family unit as a whole?

3. Imagine it is a year from now and you are reflecting on all the meaningful and fun-filled family times you have had together. What did you do that was new and different to ensure that each family member values the time spent together as a family? How were we able to create these special family times?

A Peaceful Family: Acceptance, Love and Support

A peaceful home is a one where there is a sense of connectedness, mutual sense of love, support and respect for each other. It is a home where the family members listen to one another, make time to talk about and understand differences, communicate respect and love, affirm each other, focus on strengths, and use language that builds up the other and the family. A peaceful home builds a peaceful family, where children and adults are ready to go out into the world to help create a peaceful community, school, workplace, and world.

1. Think about a time in your life when you experienced love, support and acceptance within your family. Tell me about it. What was happening? Who was involved? What was it about you and those around you that led to this sense of peacefulness and connectedness? How did that experience impact your life?

2. When you think about creating peace in your life and within your family, what do you value most about yourself as a peacemaker?

3. Imagine it is a year from now, and your friends notice how peaceful and supportive your family and home have been recently. What are you doing that is new and different that leads your friends to notice and comment on this?

Solid Sibling Relationships: Love, Care and Respect

One question we hear from parents around the world is, "How do we help brothers and sisters get along?" There has been much written on sibling rivalry – now let's spend some time thinking and talking about sibling love, care and respect. On what we focus our energy becomes our reality. If we focus attention on the times in our children's lives when they are getting along, being kind, and being cooperative with each other, we will get more of that behavior. Helping children get along with each other is a day-to-day endeavor and needs constant attention. How do we notice, pay attention to and acknowledge those special moments when our children show love, care and respect for one another?

1. Think about your relationships with your brothers and sisters. If you were an only child, think back to close friends and cousins with whom you spent a good amount of time. Tell me a story about a time when you felt loved, cared for, or respected by your brother or sister (cousin or friend). What was happening? What did your parents or other adults do to nurture this sense of support and connection between you and your siblings?

2. Now think of a time when you were called upon to support and care for a sibling during a very happy occasion or a challenging one. How did you respond? What do you value about yourself in that situation?

3. Imagine it is your assignment to introduce three ways to support and show respect for your siblings. What are some things that you could introduce into your family to make everyday a day of respect and love?

The Wisdom of Our Children

From their words to their actions, their wisdom shows up in many surprising, funny, and memorable ways, humbly reminding us adults of how much we could learn if we just listened and observed a bit more closely. When we pay attention everyday to the special qualities of our children, we can learn so much. When we take time to see our children and family members with new eyes, with appreciative eyes, and when we take time to listen and learn from them, amazing things can happen. Our children can teach us so much about themselves, the world, how they see and understand the world around them, and even about ourselves.

1. Reflecting on the many insightful, sometimes comical, surprising and witty ways in which your child's wisdom has "shown up", tell me a story about something your child said or did that made you take notice, smile, or want to give a compliment. Describe the situation.

2. What does this story tell you about your child? What admirable qualities does it reveal about him/her?

3. What does this story reveal to you about yourself, as a parent?

4. What wishes or hopes do you have for your child in sharing her wisdom and special qualities as she grows and enters the world?

5. What can you do more of or differently to further nurture your child's wisdom and other admirable qualities?

Celebrating the Best of Our Loved Ones

When people celebrate a special occasion, one of the greatest gifts we can give them is our appreciation. We can take time during the celebration to honor and celebrate the family member on their special day. Below is a set of questions that may help you begin this conversation. You can choose other topics related to the milestone you are celebrating. Have fun, be creative and explore the very best of the family member and his/her life.

We gather with family and friends to celebrate milestones (birthdays, confirmation, bar/bat Mitzvahs, graduations, anniversaries) in our lives. These are wonderful opportunities to share memorable moments, offer appreciations, and capture the positive qualities of the family members being celebrated. Let's share stories that honor and celebrate this person's life.

1. Please share with me a story of an experience you've had with (person's name) that is a high point moment for you. A time when you learned or validated how special (name) is. A time where you had fun or spent a special, memorable moment together. It could be a funny story or moving story. Tell me about that moment/experience. What happened? What was it about that time that stands out for you as a special time with (name)?

2. What do you value most about (name)? What do you appreciate most about (name)?

3. What are the qualities that help (name) shine, those qualities that make (name) the very special person he/she is?

4. What is your greatest hope for (name) as he/she enters the next phase of his/her life, or the next year?

Chapter 6

Launching: Letting Go, Going Forth

*The greatest truth must be recognition that in every man,
in every child is the potential for greatness.*
— Robert Kennedy

*I have found the best way to give advice to your children
is to find out what they want and then advise them to do it.*
— Harry S Truman

In every family there is a dynamic dance between parents and children. It involves incremental acts of letting go on the part of the parents, and small and large steps toward independence on the part of the kids. This process begins as early as a parent separates from his or her baby for the first time, and repeats as the children begin to differentiate themselves as independent individuals in their own right. For both parents and children these are sometimes bittersweet moments – joyful for what the children can become and at the same time, wistful for the dependence that will be left behind. In healthy families a new kind of interdependence develops that lasts a lifetime.

One of my initial responses to AI (Appreciative Inquiry) was to talk to my son, who was heading off to college for the first time, about the best things in his life. He reminisced about his happiest growing-up memories, his most cherished accomplishments, the gifts and skills he has developed, and some of his dreams for the future. Parents taking the opportunity to do the same for an hour a month, or even once a year, will discover a powerful tool for dissolving the stubborn generation gap so many families suffer.

— Paul Chaffee – *Unafraid of the Light*, Dec, 1997

What we see from this story is the power of the positive question. By asking our children to explore with us the very best of their past, they feel more confident about moving into the future. Transitions are hard – for everyone. As the parent suggests, don't wait until your son or daughter is heading off to college to explore the best experiences of their life. Do it often and with great sincerity and interest.

The questions that follow can contribute to making the dynamic dance you do with your family members a celebration. They may be especially helpful in times of transition toward independence.

New Beginnings

In our lives we experience many "first days" – at a new school, job, camp, class. There is the very first time we leave the safety of our family life to go to school and then in every year thereafter there is a first day. The excitement of that day can be overshadowed by fear of the unknown OR it can be full of wonder and anticipation.

1. Think back to some of your "first days". Tell me about one or two of these moments. What made them an exciting time for you? What were some of the fun ways you and your family prepared for those days?

2. Sometimes we have special ways of coping with separation that make it easier. What kinds of rituals or practices can you recall engaging in as you or your child got ready for that first day of school or going off to summer camp for the first time? Whose idea was it? What did you do? What makes you smile as you recall those times?

3. As you imagine the perfect "first day" for your child, what do you see happening? What do you hope they will experience?

The First Day of School

The first day of school is a special time in the lives of children and a memorable moment for adults. Going to school is an enormous privilege. The first day of school sets in motion a lifetime of learning – not only in the formal classroom setting, but also from school friends and foes alike. As with many other firsts in our life, the first day of school carries both positive anticipation and anxiety.

1. The first day of school each year is a very special time. Think back to some of your "first days" of school. Tell me about a particularly memorable one. What made it an exciting time for you? What were some of the fun ways you and your family prepared for that day?

2. Sometimes that first day of school might feel a bit scary. Can you remember how you were able to bravely overcome any fear you might have had? What about you made you brave? Were there others – friends, sisters or brothers – who helped you? How have you helped your friends or younger siblings enjoy the first day of school?

3. As you imagine the perfect first day of school, what do you see happening? What do you hope you will experience? How can you contribute to others' perfect first day of school?

First Love

Being in love for the first time (or "like" as with our younger children), whenever it happens, is a magical moment in time. As sweet as it is, it marks one of those times when you are operating outside of the familiar family milieu. No matter how old you are, a new love asks that both parents and children behave in new ways in relationship to each other and to the new "love".

1. Think back on that magical moment of your own first love, when you were in love (like) for the first time. Sometimes just thinking about that special person gave you butterflies in your stomach and when you were together nothing else seemed to matter. Think about your "first love". Tell me about it. What feelings stand out for you? What made it a special time for you?

2. Being in love often brings out the best in us and in others. What do you value most about yourself in this first love relationship? What do you value most about how your family supported you through this experience?

3. As you contemplate your child enjoying that first love experience, what do you hope for them? How would you hope to support them? What will make you most proud of yourself and your child during this first love experience?

Being Responsible and Making Good Choices

Life always presents us with challenges and the need to make decisions about right and wrong. Growing up means learning to make good choices, even when other people make different choices. Sometimes the choices are small, like which movie to see. Other times we are faced with bigger decisions, such as whether or not to have a sexual relationship, whether or not to smoke or use drugs, whether or not to join a gang, or break the law. Even decisions about how to use the internet and for whom to vote are big decisions as we are growing up.

There are always times when we have to choose between what is right for us and our family and what might feel wrong, or is illegal or not safe. Just because our friends choose to do something dangerous or foolish does not mean we have to do it. The ability to make decisions that are both healthy and in the best interest of everyone involved is important for our family and our community's well being.

1. Tell me about a time in your life when you felt proud of the decision you made to choose the right path or right thing to do. It might have been a time when the group you were with was engaging in an activity that was uncomfortable for you, illegal, or against your values. What was happening? What was it like for you? What was the result of your decision?

2. Thinking back on that experience, what was it about you that helped you make the right choice? What was it about the people around you that helped in making this decision?

3. What do you value most about your decision? What do you value most about the way you made that decision? What was it about you and your values that helped you make the right decision for you and your family?

4. Imagine now that it is five years later. Much has happened in your life and in your family's life. What are some of the important choices you have made in this time?

5. What can you start doing today that will send you on this path? What help might you need from those people who are important to you – your friends, parents, siblings, cousins? What can you do when you are confronted with a difficult situation that needs for you to make a good choice?

6. Imagine now that you are making choices and decisions with a sense of responsibility. You have shown that you can be trusted to make the right decisions when confronted with a difficult choice. What do you see happening? How do you know that this is happening?

7. What three things can we do everyday to encourage our family members to make choices and decisions that are healthy and nurturing?

8. What can we do to nurture a sense of inner strength to make the tough choice at the right time?

Terrific Teens

The teenage years epitomize the image of "letting go, going forth". For parents, it is the beginning of the long process of letting go of control over our children's lives. For our children, the exciting process of becoming independent really begins to take shape. This period of launching can be fraught with conflict, or it can create opportunities for deep conversation and shared meaning. Here are some questions that can help lead to the building of a new relationship between teen and parent as this transition takes place.

1. Being a teenager can be scary and exciting at the same time.

    a. For the parent: Think back when you were a teenager. What were some of the highlights of that time in your life?

    b. For the teenager: What have been some of the highlights for you so far? What was happening? Who was involved? What made those times especially exciting and meaningful?

2. During the teenage years, what did you (do you) value most about the person you were (are) becoming? What were (are) your best qualities? In what ways were (are) they demonstrated? What did (do) you value most about your support from your parents or siblings or other important people in your world then?

For the Parent:
3. Imagine now that you have the most terrific teens living in your family. What is it like? How is their new independence manifested? What kinds of conversations do you cherish having with them? What most makes you smile with pride as you watch them with friends, family and at school?

For the Teenager:
4. Imagine it is many years from now and you are a parent of teenagers. What do you value most about your relationship with them? How do you best support their growing independence? About what are you most proud in relation to your terrific teens?

License to Drive – Responsibilities & Rewards

With a driver's license come many responsibilities and rewards. The more responsible a person is – to oneself, to fellow passengers, to the road and to ongoing traffic – in using his/her license to drive, the more rewards that can be reaped – from parents, insurance companies, and the community at large in which you drive.

1. Tell me about your very first driving experience being behind the wheel of a car. Who was with you, what car/truck did you drive, and where were you going? What key learnings or insights stand out for you? How did it make you feel?

2. What most excites or fascinates you about having a driver's license? What rewards and/or privileges are you most looking forward to gaining?

3. As an experienced *passenger* to another driver (be it a trusting adult, parent or friend behind the wheel), what specific "rules of the road" would you expect a responsible driver to live by for you (and others) to feel safe?

4. Imagine it's one year from now and you've obtained your license to drive, along with the many responsibilities and rewards that go with it. Your parents, friends, and fellow passengers trust you to be one of the best, most responsible drivers ever known to them. What specific qualities about you and your driving have led others to feel this way about you? At its best, what do all the responsibilities and rewards of driving look like?

5. As your parents *let go* and trust you to sit behind the wheel, what is one step you can take immediately that will engender responsibility alongside the rewards and privileges of driving?

Leaving the Nest

For many, going forward and launching implies a time for moving on from the family nest – traveling, studying, or working – experiencing for oneself a world beyond the front doorstep. With this transition comes a strange dance of dependence and independence between a parent and child, not to mention a whirlwind of uncertainty, confusion, anticipation, and excitement.

1. Tell me a story about leaving home for the first time – be it travels for a vacation or student exchange, moving on to a new job or semester at college. What was that experience like – for yourself, for your parents, for other family members? As you look back on this experience, what key learnings stand out for you?

2. What do you value most about *home*, about "living in the nest" that you'd like to preserve in some way, no matter what else changes?

3. What three wishes do you have for your parent(s) as they let go and allow you to move forward in the world?

4. Imagine it's five years from now and we're reflecting back on today, grateful for the many achievements and lessons we've all gained from letting go, and how immensely happy we are for the joy and growth this time of transition brought for us. Pride, love, and hope surround us. Tell me what you see. What's happening? Of what accomplishments are you most proud? What about the future is so bright, and what steps did we take as a family to make it so?

Chapter 7

Contributing:
Being the Best for the World

In every community, there is work to be done. In every nation, there are wounds to heal. In every heart, there is the power to do it.

— Marianne Williamson

Contribute: to give, to supply, to provide, to bestow, to submit, to furnish. Imagine a world where all children learn the value of contributing to the world around them. Imagine a society where everyone gives that little extra to those in need, supplies help and assistance at the food bank, provides guidance to children in need of mentoring, bestows compliments on everyone they see, submits ideas and solutions to help the environment, and furnishes good wishes on someone going through a difficult time. Children learn a sense of compassion, a sense of integrity to do good in the world and a sense of responsibility as they grow and develop and as they see those whom they love displaying and living life with these qualities. We as parents can nurture these qualities throughout our children's lives by being role models and setting up opportunities to do good in the world.

Furthermore, as family members and friends we can encourage and support one another in doing what each loves to do. By giving of ourselves, we can hope that the world will be a better place for all. Children of all ages seek to know they that have done a good job and that they and their contributions matter.

On Sundays at dinner time, everyone in the family looks each other in the eye and appreciates them for something. It has been a real learning for the children, because they don't always get on! However, each week they have to find something to appreciate about the other and they always do, even if it is sometimes with ill grace. But sometimes the things that we appreciate about the others make them grow taller in their chairs. One Sunday, my youngest child (a daughter in a household with two older brothers) was going through a particularly difficult and ornery period. She couldn't have been more than eight or nine at the time. We had been to church that morning and she found 10 pence in her pocket which was a lot of money given that she only got 25 pence a week for pocket money. At church when they came around with the collection plate, she took the money I had given her for the collection AND also that 10 pence in her pocket and put it all in the dish. That evening when it came time to do "appreciates" as we call them, I appreciated her for sharing what she had with others and for sharing such a large portion of that money. I noticed that she rose inches in her seat at that moment and the most wonderful smile crossed her face!

Shared by Tricia Lustig, with permission

Teaching our children the value of giving and contributing to the world can take many forms. The mother in this story was able to compliment her daughter for donating her money to a good cause. The child learned that "giving" is something to be appreciated.

What follows are questions to explore the times in our lives when we can and do contribute to the world in a positive, constructive way. They are great questions for exploring the history of your family and helping family members learn that it is in their "genes" to make a contribution to their family, community and world at large.

Commitment to Community –
Giving Back and Making a Difference

Strong communities start with committed families who want to make a difference to the world beyond their front doorstep. When families and neighbors dedicate their time and resources to make their community cleaner, safer, more fun and more inclusive – engaging everyone, regardless of background, age or income – caring becomes infectious and everyone stands to prosper. Best of all, our children are inspired to be the change they most want to see in the world – for their community, for their family, for themselves – to think globally while acting locally.

1. Looking back at your many experiences, think of a time when you were able to make a difference for someone else – at school, with friends or family, or in our community (boy/girl scouts, church/synagogue, youth group). Consider a time when making a difference made you feel especially proud and helpful. What happened? Who was involved, and what results/outcomes were achieved? Please tell me the story.

2. What key strengths and talents do you have that allow you to make a difference in your community? What do you value most about our family's role in strengthening our community?

3. Imagine it is one year from today and our family is making a difference in our community, perhaps even more than you thought possible. Our neighbors have come together and our community is becoming stronger, more engaged, and having fun together. We're all flourishing. Describe what is happening. What's new? What did it take to get to this point? What did you contribute in particular?

Celebrating Diversity: It's Ok to be Different!

Everyday we meet people who look, dress, eat, talk, walk, ride, dance, pray, and play differently than ourselves – and that's ok! More than ok, it's *terrific*, because we each have something special and unique to give to the world in which we live.

1. Tell me about a time when you met someone different from yourself – whether in our community (at school, on the playground, on the bus), or farther away (such as during one of our family trips). Tell me the story. What qualities did you notice about the other person that made him/her special and unique? What qualities do you suspect the other person noticed about you?

2. Why do you think it's important for people to be different?

3. Of what qualities (strengths, talents, values) about yourself are you most proud? How do these qualities "show up" at school? At home? With friends?

4. When we accept, appreciate and value the many differences and diversities around us, how does this contribute to the world being the best it can be?

5. What wishes do you have for the world in valuing and celebrating differences? What might our world look like – what would be new, different, better – if these wishes were to come true?

6. What's one small step you could take today that would support those wishes coming true – for you, for our family, for the world?

Honoring Heritage

Our heritage is our identity, our daily and ceremonial traditions, our unique but shared sense of "we". Like thread to a quilt, our heritage sews stories of the past into the present, darning a legacy, bequests of culture and customs to be honored for generations to come. Honoring the best of our heritage helps us bring forward those stories that contribute to the world of which we most want to be a part.

1. Reflecting on the many traditions, customs and ways of living and being that make up your cultural heritage – at home and in our community – tell me about a time when you felt most proud to belong to your heritage. What happened? Who was there? What about this experience makes it stand out for you as *special*?

2. Let's talk a moment about some of the things you value deeply about yourself, your identity, and your cultural heritage.

   • What do you value most about yourself as a person – the qualities, habits, rituals, and experiences that make you, YOU?

   • What do you value most about your cultural heritage? What do you want to see preserved no matter what else changes?

3. As we move into the future, what wishes do you have for your children, your children's children, and your grandchildren's children in lifting up and honoring heritage? How can this contribute to helping the world be the best for all people?

4. What steps are you willing to take – small or large – that will further honor, celebrate, and preserve your heritage for generations to come?

Fostering Inclusion & Commitment

At its best, inclusion brings together people to meaningfully contribute to – and have a voice in – addressing a challenge or opportunity at hand. Engaged, included persons *commit* to what they help to create. They work together to build bridges and realize dreams with a connectedness and shared ownership that is energizing, affirming, and enduring.

1. Please tell me a story about a time when you felt most included – a BEST experience of working with others (your family, friends, colleagues, or community members) to achieve something special. Who was there? What happened? What were the outcomes – what was achieved because of inclusion? How did this make you feel?

2. Recognizing that inclusion can mean different things to different people, what does inclusion mean to you? Why is it important?

3. What wishes do you have for fostering inclusion in our home, in our neighborhood, in our community, in our world?

4. What steps can you and I take to foster this inclusion and commitment in all that we do? What examples come to mind?

Caring for the Earth

Earth Day and Earth Week come once a year, however, everyday we can work to protect, honor and take care of our global home – the Earth. We have been given the gift of sky, water, land, animals, mountains, lakes, oceans. Nature is all around us and what we do to care for the Earth tells us a lot about who we are as a people.

1. Think about all the things you do on a daily basis that contribute to keeping the Earth and our environment healthy and alive. Tell me about a few of them.

2. Now, think about a time when you did something bold, something big, that you felt was your way of saying, "I love the Earth and I want to take care of it." Tell me about that time. What was happening? What did you do? What led you to doing that? Who else was involved? How did it impact the world around you?

3. What do you value most about your participation in that experience? How can you create more opportunities like that?

4. Imagine that it is 50 years from now and the news headlines are telling us that the Earth is healthy and thriving. What was it that happened over the past 50 years to bring the Earth to this state? What did you and your family do to help with this accomplishment?

Traveling is Transformative

One of the best ways to learn about the world and to broaden your own knowledge, thinking and values is to travel in different countries. Many people visit countries other than their own. Some do it as tourists and others do it as travelers. Tourists are visitors. Travelers are learners. They value meeting people and learning about their country and culture. They may learn the language, art and music of the country. And they are willing to understand and even be of service to people facing significant challenges. Inevitably, traveling to new places changes people.

1. Tell me about a time when you traveled outside your usual world and it changed you. It might have been as simple as going from the city to the country. Or it might have been traveling to a whole new country.

2. What was it about that experience that made it a powerful opportunity for you?

3. How did you change? What was significant about this change that contributed to you becoming the person you are today?

4. If you could now travel anywhere in the world, where would you go? Tell me about your hopes and dreams for that experience.

Chapter 8

Tough Times: From Problem to Opportunity

There is great comfort and inspiration in the feeling of close human relationships and its bearing on our mutual fortunes – a powerful force, to overcome the "tough breaks" which are certain to come to most of us from time to time.

— Walt Disney

What we look for, we find. As parents we owe it to our children and to ourselves to look for the positive in everything. No matter how challenging it may seem, the "positive" is there if we are willing to look for it.

Often when tough times arise we are so focused on what could go wrong or is going wrong that we are not able to see the hopeful, the possible, and the good that can come from the challenging time. We have difficulty imagining that any good can come when we are embedded in the tough times. We spiral down further and further, often clinging to the excuse that we're protecting ourselves (and our loved ones) from a bout with disappointment. But if we imagine disappointment, we knowingly and unknowingly look for evidence that it exists, that even more disappointment is just around the bend. In short, we become our own self-fulfilling prophecy.

Amanda's daughter, a pianist, had been practicing for an upcoming piano competition that was several levels higher than she normally competes. For the sake of sparing the young girl significant disappointment, both Amanda and the piano teacher delicately told her over and over that she would not likely win. There were many more talented, more experienced pianists entering the competition than she. This was a competition that was a challenge and winning was not the likely outcome. Amanda and the piano teacher wanted to keep her daughter's expectations realistic. After hearing over and over for several weeks how she was not going to win, she finally said to Amanda, "I am sick and tired of hearing about how I am not going to win. I want to focus on doing my best." Amanda and her daughter then sat down to talk about what it would take to prepare for the contest so that she could perform her very best. She asked her about what successful practices looked like, what successful performances looked like, and they set out a strategy to prepare for the competition.

It's a good thing that Amanda's daughter listened to her heart. Despite the protective shields of caution and the piano competition she did not win but received excellent marks, the talented and determined young pianist was recently accepted into the Denver School of Performing Arts.

To this day, she immensely loves playing the piano.

— Shared by Amanda Trosten-Bloom

Imagine how the outcome of the story above might have been different had the young girl listened to her mother and piano instructor. Imagine if she focused only on what losing would look like, and how unmotivated she would have been to practice and earn her way to a seat at the Denver School of Performing Arts. As Henry Ford so simply stated, "Whether you think you can, or think you can't, either way you're right."

By seeking the positive and keeping the focus on what was most valued, the more desired outcome can be realized. This is true of every situation, every problem or challenge, large or small.

The significance of choice in dealing with especially tough times is depicted in the story of a Native American grandfather telling his grandson about the many tragedies of his life. He shared how there were two wolves in his soul, each of them fighting for his heart. One wolf was angry, full of rage for the pain and oppression suffered by his people. The other wolf was compassionate, merciful, and hopeful for the generations to come. When the grandson asked which wolf won the battle for his heart, the grandfather replied, "It depends on which one I feed."

No matter the situations brought upon us in life, we all have a choice in choosing how to deal with them; we all have a choice in deciding to which wolf we want to tend, and no person – no situation – can take that choice away from us, no matter how dire the circumstances.

The questions in this chapter are designed to help families not only look for the positive, but to find comfort and healing during tough times – to be choice-full in looking for and realizing the most desirable outcome. It is important to note that seeking the positive doesn't always come easy when challenges arise, and that's okay. Timing is everything in being ready for these conversations, and people should feel like they have permission to talk about things that hurt.

It's important to listen to and honor people's feelings, positive or negative – for them to experience being heard. If the hurt or sorrow is a major source of their energy, you are not likely to get them to speak to (let alone see) the positive until they get the bad feelings out. Listen actively, but refrain from taking it in and losing your own capacity to be appreciative. Keep a caring, but affirmative spirit. From there the foundation is laid for more hopeful and choice-full conversations around what could be and what might be in order to begin paving the way for healing – and even triumph – in tough times.

Navigating Through Tough Times

During the course of our lives we inevitably encounter tough times when we are challenged beyond what we think we can handle. The range of family challenges may mean coping with the suicide of a loved one, supporting a child with an eating disorder, or living with an alcoholic parent. In spite of all the possible difficulties we might face, we often manage to rise above them and even grow stronger as a result.

1. Think of a time when you faced a very difficult challenge in your family. Think of a time when you were really proud of the various ways you handled the adversity and were stretched beyond what you thought were your limits. What was happening? Who was involved? What was it in you that allowed you to be successful? What did others do to overcome the difficult challenge?

2. Without being humble, what do you value most about yourself during that tough time? What are your greatest qualities on which you can fall back on? For what do others rely on you?

3. What were the greatest qualities your family displayed in dealing with this situation?

4. Imagine it is several years into the future and you are encountering another family challenge. How have you leveraged these personal and family attributes that allow you to make it through tough times? What are you doing personally to support other family members or friends?

Bouncing Back from Disappointing Relations

Sometimes in life our relationships take a turn that leave us feeling disappointed, sad, or even offended and hurt. We may want to retreat and abandon the relationship – to pretend it no longer exists, or that it never was there to begin with. If we dig deep enough, however, we may find a yearning to make things better – to learn from the mistakes and get things back on the right track – if not to benefit this relationship, then to benefit new relationships we build going forward.

1. Think of a time when you bounced back from a disappointing relationship, a time when, in spite of feeling sad or hurt, you were able to find the courage and strength to make things better – for yourself and (where possible) for the other person. Please tell me the story. What has this experience taught you – about yourself, about friendship, about forgiveness?

2. What strengths do you have in yourself that helped you move beyond this difficult time?

3. What wishes do you have for yourself as you enter new relationships going forward?

4. What steps are you going to take to make these wishes a reality?

It's Okay to Cry

Being sad and grieving is a natural part of letting go. Endings are sad. Whether it's the end of a relationship, the death of a family member or friend or even the end of a great school year, it's natural to be sad. And it's okay to cry. Whenever we have a loss, an ending or a letting go in our life, we will have feelings. Expressing our feelings in healthy ways is an important part of life. Sharing our feelings with family and friends we trust is good for us, and it strengthens our bonds with them. What ever the situation, if you feel sad, it's okay to let people know and it's okay to cry.

1. Tell me about a time when you felt sad. What was the situation? What about it was sad for you?

2. How did you express your sadness? Did you cry? Who else was there and what did they do to accept your sadness?

3. How did you feel after you cried?

4. Tell me about a time when you supported another person who was sad. How did you show your love and support? How did you let them know it was okay to cry?

5. How did supporting this person make you feel?

Stepping Out of an Abusive Relationship

Sometimes relationships become abusive and turn into a situation where words, and in some cases touch, are repeatedly hurtful. This is especially difficult to bear when we care deeply for the person hurting us. It takes much strength – much confidence and self-determination – to step out of the relationship and climb to higher, safer ground. We may not know these strengths to exist in ourselves, especially at times when we are feeling sad and weak, but if we look deep enough, these strengths and more are sure to be found. And often, the strength comes from reaching out to others for help.

1. Recall a relationship that you have had or are currently in where you have felt supported, loved, and nurtured. What did (does) that relationship look like? Tell me about it.

2. Think of a person with whom you have felt completely safe, assured of his or her care for your health, safety and well-being. What story or person comes to mind? Please describe it in detail. What did other person do? What did you do? How did this make you feel?

3. Without being humble, what do you value most about yourself? What key strengths, gifts, or qualities do you bring to a loving, nurturing relationship?

4. Given your responses above, what does it take – what are the core building blocks (for yourself and for the other) for nurturing a safe, loving, enduring relationship?

5. Now, thinking about the abusive relationship you are in, what strengths can you bring forth to move yourself away from this situation? What resources do you have, on what other relationships can you rely to help you move away from the abuse?

6. In thinking about moving away from the abusive relationship, what wishes do you have for yourself to move forward? What bold changes will you need to make to ensure all relationships in which you engage are loving and nurturing – for you and everyone involved?

Seeking the Positive:
Being Honest in Difficult Circumstances

Positive attributes of honesty and trust are sometimes met with apprehension and fear – fear of vulnerability, of being let down or letting down another; and yet, it is said that, "what goes around, comes around." If honesty and trust are indeed positive attributes of which we want more, we need to make more to go around. A child that learns to nurture honesty and trust at home will also learn to nurture those values at school, in the community, and for the world.

1. Think of a time when you were forthcoming about something that you feared would disappoint the other person (your parent, your spouse, a relative or friend). What happened and what did it take for you to muster up the courage to be that open and honest? What did the other person do to make it safe to do so? Please describe the situation in as much detail as possible.

2. What strengths did you find in yourself that enabled you to be honest and forthcoming, in spite of the difficult circumstances?

3. What happened as a result of the situation? What was the outcome? What did that teach you?

4. Imagine history repeating itself and you find yourself in similar circumstances. What might you do differently to produce an even more satisfying outcome? In other words, what learnings do you have now, that you didn't have then, that would be put to good use?

From Setbacks to Stepping Forward: Coming to Terms with Differences in an Important Relationship

Being in a relationship with another person often challenges us to hear and acknowledge a different perspective or point of view. We are especially called upon to honor our differences as the relationship evolves to a new place or encounters setbacks along the way.

1. Describe a time in your relationship when you encountered a setback that required both of you to draw on your best skills and assets to jointly meet the challenge. What happened? What did each of you contribute to the positive outcome?

2. What did you most value about yourself in this situation? What did you most appreciate about the other person?

3. In even the best of relationships, there are times when we disagree and see things differently, and yet we are able to work toward a mutually acceptable outcome. During the many successful years of your relationship, what were some strategies that allowed you to come to terms with your differences. What did compromise look like? How did you get there?

4. Imagine that it is five years from now. When you look back at this difficult period in your lives, about what will you be most proud that you did for yourself? For the other person in the relationship? For the others who care about you?

Risky Business:
Experimenting with Sex, Drugs,
and other Risky Behaviors

Life's journey is filled with forks in the road – choice points where we're challenged in a split moment to decide between right and wrong. Sometimes what feels right at the time could actually be quite risky, or wrong altogether – bad for our health, our bodies, others and our safety, or our conscience. No one consistently chooses the right way all the time; some times we choose intelligently, and other times we don't. All make for great learning along the way.

1. Tell me about a time when you met a "fork in the road" and had to choose between right and wrong (or risky). Maybe it was a choice point for telling the truth or lying; experimenting with sex, drinking, or drugs; or doing something potentially dangerous (to you or to others). What happened? Who was involved? What choices did you make, and what came about as a result?

2. What lessons did you gain from that experience? What do you know now that perhaps you didn't know then?

3. If given the opportunity to relive that experience, what would you do differently? What would you do the same?

4. Moving forward, what wishes do you have for yourself or for others who meet similar forks in the road? What support do you need (from myself, others) to ensure that those wishes can come true?

Triumph Over Peer Pressure:
Putting Our Values First

Sometimes people we respect and admire invite us to do things we don't want to, and even go so far as to put our friendship with them on the line. We find ourselves having to choose between doing what might please others, versus doing what is true to our deeply held principles – what we know to be "right". When we choose to put our principles first, we exude confidence, uncompromising strength and self-respect. This underlines the importance of loving and respecting yourself before you can love and respect another.

1. Tell me about a time when you made a choice because it was right for you, regardless of what other persons (whom you greatly respected) wanted you to do. What happened? Who was there? What came about as a result? How did this choice make you feel?

2. What standards, principles, or values does this experience reveal as fundamentally important to you – core values you want preserved no matter what? Further, what strengths do this experience reveal about yourself that perhaps you didn't previously notice?

3. What does it mean to say "you have to love and respect yourself before you can love and respect another"? Where does this maxim ring true in the story you just shared?

4. What wishes do you have for yourself in handling future challenges, like this one and others, with still greater confidence and ease?

Chapter 9

Aging Gracefully

"Live the life you've dreamed"

— David Thoreau

"No wise man ever wished to be younger"

— Jonathan Swift

Just when we think we have life figured out it starts to change. The process of aging shows up without warning. For some, the experience of aging begins with a few gray hairs, or a grandchild's call, "Gama". For others it comes with an injury, a loss of a childhood friend to cancer, or an invitation to join AARP. For family members the experience of aging may mean watching parents, grandparents and elder aunts and uncles change shape, lose capacities and become forgetful. For many others it means sharing time with joyful parents who volunteer at their church, mosque or synagogue, who go to the health club regularly, or who take classes at the local college. The process of aging, like all other times in life, can be a time of joy and vitality, a time of giving back to society, and of continuous learning. The questions in this chapter can help you discuss aging with your partner, your parents and your children. When aging gracefully is a family conversation, everyone benefits.

When my friends invited me to visit and to meet their 105 year old father my heart and soul leapt at the chance to meet an elder who was joyful, content and flourishing. My own mother had just turned 81 and was not a happy elder. Her suffering, in an odd way, was bringing our family together. However, for me, it was just wearing me out. My self-talk about aging was getting more and more negative. I needed a vibrant positive role model.

Meeting David was an incredible gift, more than I could have imagined. He was a delightful human being, a deeply spiritual man. He welcomed me into his home, a one-bedroom apartment where he lived alone and cooked for himself. His son and daughter-in-law lived four floors up in their own apartment. As we sat together I learned about David and he asked me a number of questions about my life and my wishes. Oh, the wonder of meeting a man who was sincerely curious at 105. And he had suggestions for me, what to do to fulfill my greatest hopes and dreams.

I learned that David's synagogue was on the first floor of his apartment building. He attended services twice daily. Each time he left his apartment he was greeted by neighbors, young and old. He always returned their greetings with a pat on the head, or a tap on the shoulder, and a few words of blessing. He was the resident spiritual teacher, an adored and adoring wise one. Before I left for the evening David said a prayer over me. Meeting David changed my thinking about getting older.

As the evening progressed I could hear the question in my mind shift. It went from, "How can I avoid the helplessness that seems to come with aging?" to, "How can I begin now to accept and enjoy my aging process and to cultivate my spiritual strength to live a long, healthy and contributing life?" As my self-talk changed so did my outlook on aging.

Opportunities to meet and spend time with elders are one of the best ways to shape our own images for positive aging. When school children spend time with elders playing, hearing stories and working side by side, they not only learn about history, they also form respectful and hopeful images of aging. As the story above illustrates, the questions we ponder about aging – our own and others – greatly influence how we age. The more positive our images of aging the more likely we will age gracefully.

The following questions can serve as conversation starters for you and your family members about issues important to aging. Since it will happen to all of us, we might as well talk about aging and learn what matters most to family members in the process.

Role Models of Positive Aging

The visions we hold about aging influence us. The more positive our images, the more likely we will age gracefully. As more and more people cross over from middle age to be elders, we have more opportunities to see people, in our families and in public, who are role models of positive aging. They are healthy and productive, continue to care for their families and society, express themselves creatively and generously pass their wisdom and knowledge on to younger people.

1. Who are your role models of positive aging? Please tell me about 2 to 3 people. They may be alive or have passed at this time. Please share with me a memorable moment when you shared a time with one of these important people. What was happening? Who was there? How did the experience impact you and your outlook on life?

2. What is (was) it about each of them that make them role models of positive aging for you?

3. Now, tell me a story about a time when one of them shared their wisdom with you. What was the situation and what did you learn from him or her? What was it about this person that has "rubbed off" on you?

4. As you think of yourself as an older person, what image do you have for how you will be a role model for positive aging? What hopes and dreams do you have for yourself as you imagine yourself aging gracefully?

Lessons from Our Grandparents

For many of us, time with our grandparents was, or still is, a special time. Not only do grandparents seem to love us unconditionally, they also have a way about them that lets us lovingly know what is right and what is wrong. They convey their values by the way they treat us, in special phrases or through stories they tell us.

1. Share with me a story that tells of a special moment between you and your grandparent(s) when you learned a valuable lesson. What was happening? How did this come about? What did you take away from that experience?

2. Think about all that you have learned from your grandparents. What were the key messages they gave you?

3. Is there a phrase or saying that your grandparents repeated that you have as a reminder of how to behave or how to do something? What is it?

4. Tell me about a really fun time you shared with a grandparent. When was it and what made it really fun?

5. What did you learn from your grandparents about being "good grandparents"?

Living with Limitations

With aging comes limitations and decline. It is inevitable. The health and well-being of elders depends on how they, and the people around them, handle their limitations. Caring for people who are living with limitations can be challenging. Sometimes they let you help them, sometimes they don't.

Let's explore your ideas on how to show care for people who live with limitations. Think about people you know who have limitations. They may be physical, mental or emotional. Whatever it is, they can't do what they once did, or what others do easily.

1. Tell me about one person who is limited in some way and who you really admire. They may be a younger person or an older person. What is his or her limitation? Why do you admire him or her?

2. Now, think of a time when giving and accepting care and assistance helped to nurture your relationship with this person. It may have only happened once, or it may happen frequently. Tell me about it. What happened and how? What do you value most about your role in this relationship? What was it about the other person that fosters a mutual relationship of care?

3. As you get older and may be unable to do everything for yourself, what kind of help and care would feel good and respectful for you? How do you see yourself accepting this care?

Elder Care: A Family Affair

Aging is the other end of the life spectrum from birth and yet caring for an elder sometimes seems like caring for a newborn. As we age we often need help with even the most basic life activities like dressing, eating and going out for a walk. There are many forms of elder care available from assisted living in an elder community to moving in with the family. No matter what form of care is selected, family members will still be called upon for love, compassion and often hands-on help.

1. Tell me about a time when your family or another family you know, pulled together to care for someone needing full-time care; it may have been a long time ago or recently. What was the situation? Who was involved and what did they do?

2. What do you value most about the way you were able to contribute to this caring situation? What does this tell you about your family's strengths and resources?

3. Imagine now that you are the elder for whom care is being given. Imagining the very best situation possible, what is happening? How does your family come together to care for you?

4. With this image in mind, as your family members get older, how do you envision your family will care for them? What might you do now to prepare for this time?

It's Never Too Late

As we age we often find ourselves thinking about things we have always wanted to do, but have not done yet. It is important to realize that it is never too late to fulfill your dreams. People have run their first marathon in their 70's, gone back to school and graduated in their 80's, and had their first art exhibit in their 90's. Aging often affords opportunities for learning, travel and creative expression that were not available earlier in life. I am curious about what you want to do, be and achieve in the next decade.

1. There are always things we've dreamed about doing or experiencing throughout our life that we have not yet done. What are some of the things, small and large, that you would still like to do?

2. Now, thinking back over your lifetime, what is one unfulfilled childhood or young adulthood dream that you still hope to fulfill? What are the first steps you need to take toward making this a reality? What will it feel like for you to do this?

3. What support do you need to realize this dream? How can your family and friends help make this dream come true?

Improbable Parenting: Parenting Our Parents

At some point during our middle years, some of us experience a sometimes subtle, occasionally dramatic change in our relationship with our parents. We become the caretakers of our parents and they become dependent upon us for emotional, financial or intellectual support. The tables have turned. How can we make this a life-giving role reversal for all involved?

1. Times of transition afford us the opportunity to bring forward the best of the past as we innovate new ways of being in relationships. Tell me a story of a time when you felt tremendously supported by your parents or an elder. What happened? Who was involved? What were the special behaviors that allowed you to feel safe and cared for?

2. What do you value most about yourself as a nurturing and caring adult? What unique contributions can you make as a caregiver for your parents or other aging people in your life that will support their needs as they become less independent?

3. Given this opportunity to care for a parent, what characteristics and strengths do you possess that you can bring to this experience?

4. Imagine now, that you are 90+ years old. You need constant care and have several caring adult children in your life who are now providing the best possible care for you. What do you see happening? How do you accept and appreciate that care? What are they doing to help you live to your fullest potential given the situation? How has your relationship grown and changed? What is it about your relationship with them that makes you feel safe and happy in your final days?

5. Think of three surprising and growth-filled outcomes of this experience.

Chapter 10

Completing: Elegant Endings

Other things may change us, but we start and end with the family.

— Anthony Brandt

This phase in the cycle of family life is about closure and at the same time it also contains the all important thread of continuity and the opportunity for new beginnings. Completing in this context includes critical events in family life such as separation, divorce, aging and dying. As usual, even in the midst of difficulty and pain, we have the opportunity to see these events through the lens of joy, learning, and possibility for the future. It is often during challenging times in our life that we discover an inner source of strength we never knew we had. Here are some positive questions to help you move through this phase elegantly as you honor the past and create the future of your dreams.

"Out beyond ideas of wrong-doing and right-doing,
there is a field.
I'll meet you there."

— RUMI

Sometimes, in spite of our best intentions, good things come to an end. This was true of my first marriage. We met, fell in love, gave birth to two beautiful girls and then began to grow apart. Looking back, I think ours was a "starter" marriage that simply went beyond its shelf life.

When we did divorce, we spent time imagining the brightest possible future for each of us as individuals and for our children. Being aware of the potent effect of conflict generated by litigation and the attending decimation of assets, we chose to create our own agreements that we could modify as needed. Knowing that in the future there would be recitals, team sports, graduations, weddings and grandchildren, we wanted to create an enduring sense of connection and support for our daughters and to demonstrate that even when families change form, there can still be love and inclusiveness.

Today, almost twenty years later, our daughters have two step parents, four step siblings and two half-siblings. On the day that our first grandchild was born, we were able to celebrate his birth together and to bear witness to the continuation of our small family and the tapestry of the larger family that our initial intentions manifested.

© Sandra Wells, 2008

As this story tells us, it is the time we spend in conversation *intentionally* that matters most, co-creating the type of relationships, family structure and life we want to live. The questions we ask shape the future for everyone involved. We can ask – what is our brokenness, what caused our unhappy ending? Or, we can ask – what are our strengths and values, what is it that we are most capable of doing to bring this chapter of our life to a close and open a new chapter full of possibility and growth?

As the questions in this chapter suggest, endings can be as simple as the end of the day or as significant as the end of life. Whatever your situation, these questions can help you open conversations that will keep the words, tears and ultimately the joy flowing.

Separation and Divorce with Intentionality

The choice to uncouple is always a difficult one, often fraught with grief, anger, drama and uncertainty about the parents' and children's future. The manner in which we choose to move on makes all the difference in the outcomes achieved for everyone involved.

Starting the appreciative conversation during such challenging, even painful times can be tricky. Some find it helpful to experiment first with oneself (such as in individual reflection and/or journal writing) and to later initiate conversations with the other spouse/partner; others are just as comfortable to launch into a paired conversation from the get go. Regardless of what works best for you, it is important to keep in mind that *people commit to what they help to create* – that the creation of a peaceful separation or divorce is only possible when everyone impacted is involved in the conversation. Just as coming together was a collaborative effort, so is moving apart.

There is a difference between "hanging in there in misery," and "living life with intention". No matter the helplessness that one often feels when coping with divorce, we are all empowered to choose the latter.

1. Think back over your life. Recall a time when you were dealing with a very difficult situation, one where the outcome was very important for moving forward. Recall a time when you dealt with this situation with an intentionality that guided the journey through this tough time. Tell me about it. What was happening? Who was involved? What did you do with intentionality that helped you through this situation?

2. Now, in thinking about an impending separation/divorce, what kind of role model do you want to be for your children as you face these difficult times? How do you want your children to think about their parents?

3. What adjectives would you like to hear your children choose as they describe their parents to others? And what behaviors might they witness for these adjectives to be truthful?

4. Given the choices you've made, what lessons are your children learning from this experience, particularly regarding relationships and resolving differences? What lessons do you want them to learn? What can you do differently to make this so?

5. Fast forward to several years from now and visualize sitting down with your children (now grown adults). You reflect aloud on the many changes that have taken place since the divorce, and how proud and grateful you are for the life you all now lead.

- What does that life look like (for yourself, for your children, for your partner)? What about it makes you especially proud and grateful? Please describe in detail what you see.

- What did you do a few years ago (present day) that helped make this life possible? What could you be doing more of, or differently, *now,* that will positively impact what you achieve moving forward?

When the Job is Done

The end of a job, a project or even a career is a time of mixed emotions. There may be relief about being done and being free of the responsibilities involved. There may be joy and celebration over the successful completion of goals and dreams. At the same time there may be sadness and confusion about what comes next. Taking time to reflect on the job, the project or the career when it was at its best can free up energy and ideas to go forward.

1. How did you get started in this job or project? Who or what attracted you to it?

2. Tell me about a highpoint experience during this job, with this project, or in your career – a time when you were really energized and at your best.

3. What made it a highpoint experience for you?

4. What did you learn in this job or on this project that had made you who you are today?

5. What about this job do you want to continue as you move on to what ever comes next in your life?

On Death and Dying:
Making the Best of Our Time Together

Opening a new door for hope and possibility doesn't always come easy when dealing with the anticipated loss of a loved one. No matter the grief or fear, we want to make the most of our precious time together, to revisit and refresh joyful stories of the past, to immortalize them in memory, and to uncover a generative, positive fuel source that will nurture and propel us into this still vague, but now more hopeful future.

As we prepare for the loss of our loved one, we have the opportunity for rich dialogue among family members about our relationships, of what we are most proud, and what our loved one's greatest hopes are for our future as we say good-bye. Being in dialogue at this time gives us the opportunity to be in reflection, to remember, and to revisit our life together.

1. Family histories carry many ups and downs, high points and low points. Think about a high point, a time of pure joy – when you felt especially proud, hopeful, and happy to belong to this very gifted, special family. What story, or memory, comes to mind? Who was involved? What stands out for you that you have carried with you until now? What strengths and unique gifts does this story reveal about our loved ones that we may not have noticed before?

2. Thinking back over your life when you were at your best, what was it that you were doing? How did that impact those around you? How do you feel now looking back?

3. Without being humble, describe the gifts which you gave to this family over the years. What are the contributions and special qualities you have offered this family that which you are most proud?

4. What makes each of your family members the greatest on earth? What do you value and appreciate most in each of them? Tell them aloud.

5. Imagine a future where your most vivid, positive dreams come true for all your loved ones – a future where your greatest hopes are realized. What does that future look like for your family? Who is doing what, and how are your loved ones going about their lives? Describe in detail the dream you have for each of them.

6. What words of appreciation, wisdom and love do you want to convey to your loved ones right now?

End-of-the-Day Reflections

The end of the day is an excellent time for us to look back on the day with our children and to bring forth the best moments, feelings and memories. Together we can recreate our experiences by highlighting them. Consider the questions below as nighttime soothers as you are bringing the day to a close. Begin by sharing specific affirmations and appreciations you have for the person with whom you are talking – recognizing a good deed, good behavior, or an image you have of that person excelling in a particular strength or talent (drawing, singing, counting to ten, reading a new book, playing nice with others). They are sure to sleep more soundly after hearing your words of encouragement, and even stand taller when they wake up the next day. Start by saying:

Today many things happened and I would like to take a few minutes with you to remember some of the highlights or best moments from today.

1. What was your favorite part about today? Tell me the story. How did it make you feel?

2. What one thing did you do today that made you feel especially proud of yourself?

3. What did you learn today that excited you (in school, with friends, at home)?

4. What are you going to dream about in your sleep?

5. What wishes do you have for an even more exciting day tomorrow? What wishes do you have for your siblings, parents, grandparents, classmates, teachers? (choose one or two)

Farewell to a Family Pet

Our beloved pets hold a very special place in the dynamics of our families. Each family member has a unique relationship with each one of our animals. Losing a pet for any reason – old age, illness or changing circumstances elicits sadness for family members of all ages. In the midst of our grieving, however, there is the opportunity to celebrate the uniqueness of our pet that is no longer with us. The questions that follow are relevant for everyone in the family and especially lend themselves to be shared among all who loved our furry friend.

1. We are all sad that (Pet's name) is no longer here with our family making us laugh and cuddling up with us. And we each have so many wonderful memories of happy times with (Pet's name). Let's each share a story about (Pet's name) which makes you laugh and smile just remembering. What was happening? Who was involved? What makes you smile the most when you think about (Pet's name)?

2. When you think about your own special times with (Pet's name), what do you value most about yourself as a friend to (Pet's name)? What is most meaningful to you about having pets in our family?

3. Imagine it is a year from now, and we have a new pet living in our family. What are you doing to care for and love our pet? How has our time with (Pet's name) helped us welcome more furry friends into our family?

Chapter 11

Closing Thoughts and Encouragement

As we live and work within the technological envelope of the twenty-first century, let us remember the relational imperative for human well-being – LOVE.
— Diana Whitney

Where appreciation is alive and generations are reconnected through inquiry, hope grows and family expands.
— David Cooperrider

Every day, every moment, we have choices to make about how we relate to our children, our spouse or partner, our siblings, our parents, our neighbors, co-workers, everyone with whom we come in contact. We can choose to focus on where others fall short of our expectations, the blame, the weaknesses, the mistakes, and the pain, or we can choose to look for the new, the hopeful, the intriguing, the exciting, the love-filled parts of our lives and relationships. What we look for, we will find. What we find will grow and expand. What grows and expands becomes our reality.

As with any new learning, the act of asking positive questions takes patience and practice. Further, it takes intentionality to choose to ask them – a choice that doesn't always come naturally. We all experience emotions of sadness, fear, confusion, and anger – feelings that make it all too easy to abandon positive intentionality.

It is in these moments that we need to call upon self-control to honor our feelings, and to honor the outcomes we most want, regardless of what we're feeling at that very moment. It's as though we push a "pause button" and, rather than spiraling down, we think about the end result we most want to achieve – and then ask ourselves, "What is the question that I can ask now that is most likely to get me/us *there*?" Let us emphasize that this is not about ignoring the problems, but rather, about reframing them and redirecting the conversation to focus on what you want for your family.

Parents often ask how to overcome the challenge of getting their teens and pre-teens to talk to them. It's important to remember that children of this age group may appear outwardly more concerned about what their peers think of them than about what their parents want to talk to them. The mere act of asking the positive question shows you care, and that alone carries much weight. Further, by repeatedly asking through an appreciative, affirmative lens, the child will learn to see the world through an appreciative lens. Our colleagues and clients from around the globe continue to remind us that Appreciative Inquiry – be it at the workplace or at home – can become a very contagious and fulfilling habit. It is one way to co-create the world in which we most want to live.

Remember Three Simple Concepts

This book is meant to be a resource, not a "how to" book. It is filled with examples of questions with the hopes that you see the patterns and will create your own questions, addressing those things that are most important in your life and family. No doubt there will be many conversations ahead where you won't have the benefit of a typed interview question from which you can read aloud and be on your way. And since memorizing this entire book of questions is just as unlikely, we offer three simple concepts as reminders and an invitation for you to create your own questions.

1. What you seek, you find more of.

The questions we ask are fateful; the more positive the question, the more positive the images and actions that follow. The choice of *what* you ask is yours exclusively.

Human beings are natural problem solvers. If the things we want and need in life appear missing (i.e. food, water, shelter, belonging), we go out and look for it. However, by looking for the problems, we become experts in what's wrong, weak, or missing altogether. We live our glass half-empty.

From our experience, when families focus on problems and "what's wrong", children and other loved ones become discouraged and less optimistic that the problems will ever go away. Often after family interventions or conversations aimed at dealing with problems, family members note how they've become more aware of the problems and how they've impacted them in an even more negative way. Further, they walk away with a clear understanding of what not to do when moving forward to prevent the problems from reoccurring, but still lack focus around what to do to achieve higher ground, not to mention enthusiasm and excitement for rolling up their sleeves and getting started.

Alternatively, when families come together to identify and study examples of when they've experienced things going well, they become energized and generate creative solutions to their challenges. They increase their capacities to affirm, to think more expansively, and to work more collaboratively in examining what's possible. Additionally, family members support the solutions and changes because they were the ones who created them.

This brings us to our second very important, and yet deceptively simple concept.

2. People commit to what they help create.

By asking the question, you take on a position of inquiry in place of advocacy, inviting the other to discover what matters, why it matters, and what it could look like at its very best. You open the door to a two (or more) way conversation that co-creates, instead of dictates, the path ahead in such a way that everyone involved is committed to getting there – because they helped create it.

It's often easy (and tempting) to put ourselves in the control seat, particularly when we're confronted with a conflict where the "should have done's" are compellingly clear in our view. More often than not, as adults, we're expected to be the experts to our younger children – to know why the sky is blue, why grass is green, and why dogs walk on four legs instead of two. However, by always being the expert – by always *telling* instead of asking – we pass up golden opportunities to nurture curiosity, cooperation, responsibility, independence, and self-discipline.

By telling the other what to do, or giving an answer, we wear the hat of solution provider, and let's face it, no matter how brilliant the solution, only the people who created it are really committed to moving it forward. From the age of two, we humans take on the "I do it!" way of life; we long to make decisions and choose actions on our own. Though telling may generate desired results from others near-term, long-term is another story; in every question there is an opportunity for the other to be part of generating ideas and possibilities. We are teaching each other the power of the positive question in co-creating the world in which we want to live.

Our daughter had become a world-class whiner at the ripe old age of three and a half. But instead of continually nagging her to stop (that is, responding with whining of our own) and use "peaceful voice", we asked her to suggest a gesture or phrase that the family could use as a signal when whining commenced. She proposed a tug on the right ear and we all agreed. Further, should the whining persist or escalate, she suggested a more verbal queue, like saying the phrase, "Wiggle! Wiggle! Wiggle!" to signal to the other person that it was time to go cool off in a place of the person's choosing, such as a temporary retreat to the bedroom, bathroom, or outside. We continue to use these signals in place of nagging, and our daughter even uses them herself when she hears nagging tension between Mommy and Daddy. Having participated in the creation of the solution, and in having opportunities to enforce the solution she helped create, she is committed to respecting what it takes to make "peaceful voice" the norm at home.

It's very frightening to think of moving away from thrones of control and advocacy as parents. We're not telling you to have a "long leash" or to let go of the leash altogether. What we are saying, however, is that by inviting the other into the conversation to co-create the solution, you're increasing your chances of cooperation and commitment from everyone involved. People of all ages are more likely to commit to what they help to create.

3. Stories honor the past and build confidence for the future.

We have found that beginning the appreciative conversation with a question that invites the others to tell their story will set the tone for further dialogue. When we explore what has been most successful in the past, related to any topic of inquiry, this gives us energy and confidence to move into the future. Keep the stories of personal and family success alive by telling them over and over. It is the stories that we remember when we look back at life, our own and the life of loved ones who have moved on. Through the power of story, we know each other and what is important to each of us and to the family as a whole. It is the stories that we create and remember together that strengthen relationships and a sense of family.

Creating Your Own Questions

When getting started, remember to first focus on the *story* you want to draw from your loved one's past. It could be 'past' as in an hour ago, or 'past' as in 20 or more years ago. Our stories of joy, happiness, and achievement reveal endless possibilities – many of them previously unnoticed – for creating the future we most desire. "Stories have wings and they fly from mountaintop to mountaintop." This Romanian proverb tells us of the powerful potential of sharing our lives with each other through story.

Follow these simple steps:

1. Ask your loved ones to share their story;

2. Probe to see what they most valued about that experience and what else can be learned from the events and experiences revealed;

3. Then invite them to share their hopes and dreams or wishes for the future – 'what could be' when things or people are at their best.

Keep the sequence, and keep it simple. Make it yours, and have fun. You are sure to open doors to new rooms in each other's hearts that no one – not even you – knew existed.

Opening Your Appreciative Eyes, Heart and Mind

We hope that this book has piqued your interest in the power of positive questions to create the reality you most want for yourself and for your family. We hope it has given you insight into how to generate even greater joy in the good times; and how to see positive possibilities and navigate choice-fully and confidently through life's challenging times. It is through appreciative dialogues that life with our families and relationships are nurtured, grown and become life-giving and fulfilling. Isn't that what family is all about?

We also hope that the questions in this book have opened your eyes – your appreciative eyes – and that you are more able and ready to see the good within your friends and family members. When you look through your appreciative eyes, what do you see in your children? When you listen with your appreciative heart, what do you notice about your spouse and your friends? When you ask questions from your appreciative mind, what do you learn about your siblings and parents?

The questions and conversations we invite within our families and friendships provide opportunities for us to co-create the world in which we most want to live. Using positive questions to share our hearts and minds with each other creates a world of love and respect. Asking questions that celebrate our relationships with one another as they grow and change creates a world of hope and optimism. Being curious about what gives life and brings joy to each other creates a world of wonder, harmony and happiness. This is the world of our dreams. We invite you to help us create it – one question at a time.

Other Books by the Authors

Appreciative Inquiry: A Positive Revolution in Change. Cooperrider, D. and Whitney, D., Berrett-Koehler Publishers, Inc. 2006.

Appreciative Team Building: Positive Questions to Bring Out the Best of Your Team. Whitney, D., Trosten- Bloom, Cherney, J. and Fry, R. iUniverse, Inc. 2004

The Appreciative Inquiry Summit: A Practitioner's Guide for Leading Large-Group Change. Ludema, J., Whitney, D., Mohr, B., and Griffin, T., Berrett-Koehler Publishers, Inc. 2003.

Appreciative Inquiry Handbook: The First in a Series of AI Workbooks for Leaders of Change. Cooperrider, D., Whitney, D., and Stavros, J., Crown Communication. 2003. Second Edition 2007.

The Power of Appreciative Inquiry: A Practical Guide to Positive Change. Whitney, D. and Trosten-Bloom, A., Berrett-Koehler Publishers, Inc. 2002.

The Encyclopedia of Positive Questions, Volume One: Using Appreciative Inquiry to Bring Out the Best in Your Organization. Whitney, D., Cooperrider, D., Trosten-Bloom, A., and Kaplin, B., Crown Communication. 2002.

Positive Approaches to Peace Building: A Resource for Innovators. Sampson, C., Abu-Nimer, M., Leibler, C. and Whitney, D., editors Washington, DC: Pact Publications. 2003

Appreciative Inquiry and Organizational Transformation: Reports from the Field. Fry, R., Barrett, F., Seiling, J., and Whitney, D., Quorum Books. 2002.

The Appreciative Organization. Anderson,H., Cooperrider, D., Gergen, K., Gergen, M., McNamee, S., and Whitney, D. Taos Institute Publications. 2001. Second Edition 2008.

Appreciative Inquiry: Foundations in Positive Organization Development. Cooperrider, D., Sorensen, P., Yaeger, T., and Whitney, D. editors Stipes Publishing, LLC. 2001.

Appreciative Inquiry: An Emerging Direction for Organization Development. Cooperrider, D., Sorensen, P., Yaeger, T., and Whitney, D. editors Stipes Publishing, LLC. 2001.

Appreciative Inquiry: Rethinking Human Organization Towards a Positive Theory of Change. Cooperrider, D., Sorensen, O., Whitney, D., and Yaeger, T. editors Stipes Publishing, LLC. 2000.

References and Resources

Armstrong, Thomas, *In Their Own Way: Discovering and Encouraging Your Child's Multiple Intelligences,* Penguin Putnam Inc.: New York, 2000.

Buck, Nancy, *Peaceful Parenting,* Black Forest Press: Chula Vista, CA, 2002.

Barrett, Frank and Fry, Ronald, *Appreciative Inquiry, A Collaborative Approach to Building Cooperative Capacity,* Taos Institute Publications, 2005.

Faye, Jim, and Cline, Foster, *Parenting with Love and Logic,* Pinon Press, 1990, updated version 2006.

Fox, Jennifer, *Your Child's Strengths: Discover them, develop them, use them,* Viking, 2008.

Jenkins, Peggy J., *Nurturing Spirituality in Children,* Beyond Words Publishing, Inc. Hillsboro, OR, 1995.

Kelm, Jacqueline, *Appreciative Living: The Principles of Appreciative Inquiry in Personal Life,* Venet Publishers, 2005.

Nelsen, Jane, *Positive Discipline,* Ballantine Books: New York, 1996.

Stavros, Jaqueline and Torres, Cheri, *Dynamic Relationships: Unleashing the Power of Appreciative Inquiry in Daily Living,* Taos Institute Publications, Chagrin Falls, OH, 2005.

Vannoy, Steven W., *The 10 Greatest Gifts I Give My Children: Parenting from the Heart,* Fireside, Simon and Schuster, Inc. New York, NY, 1994.

Watkins, Jane and Mohr, Bernard, *Appreciative Inquiry: Change at the Speed of Imagination,* San Francisco, CA: Jossey-Bass/Pfeiffer, 2001.

E-BASED Resources

Appreciative Inquiry Commons: www.Appreciativeinquiry.cwru.edu
   The worldwide portal for Appreciative Inquiry resources.

The Taos Institute: www.taosinstitute.net
   The Taos Institute is committed to exploring, developing and disseminating
   ideas and practices that promote creative, appreciative and collaborative
   processes in families, communities and organizations around the world.

Corporation for Positive Change: www.positivechange.org
   Consulting and workshops in Appreciative Inquiry, Positive Change and
   Appreciative Leadership

Innovation Partners International: www.innovationpartners.com
   IPI offers consulting, public and in-house workshops, and speaking
   engagements in Appreciative Inquiry, Strength-Based Organizations (SBO),
   Strategy, and Leadership

Appreciative Inquiry Consulting: www.AIConsulting.org
   AI Consulting, LLC offers a collaborative, strength-based approach to
   strategic change and transformation.

Positive Organizational Scholarship: www.bus.umich.edu/positive
   The Center for Positive Organizational Scholarship is committed to
   advancing research in the emerging field of Positive Organizational
   Scholarship (POS).

Appreciative Living: www.appreciativeliving.com
   At Appreciative Living, we use the foundational principles of
   Appreciative Inquiry, along with law of attraction, positive psychology, and
   other positive approaches to help you create the life of your dreams.

Endnotes

1. Munuchin, S., (1977) *Families and Family Therapy,* Harvard University Press, Cambridge, MA, p. 46.

2. Gottman, J. M. (1994). *What Predicts Divorce: The Relationship Between Marital Processes & Marital Outcomes.* New York: Lawrence Earlbaum.

3. Losada, M., and Heaphy, E. (2004) *The Role of Positivity and Connectivity in the Performance of Business Teams: A Nonlinear Dynamics Model* (p. 7), *American Behavioral Scientist,* 47 (6), pp. 740-765.

About the Authors

Dawn Cooperrider Dole is the Executive Director of the Taos Institute (www.taosinstitute.net) and the Knowledge Manager of the Appreciative Inquiry Commons (http://appreciativeinquiry.case.edu). She holds a master's degree in Education and a current teaching certification as well as a master's degree in Organization Development and Analysis. Dawn has spent the past 28 years working with youth, youth serving organizations, not-for-profits, healthcare, and schools. She consults with schools, businesses, churches and non-profits organizations using strength-based and appreciative methods for bringing about positive and collaborative change. Dawn designs and leads experiential teambuilding and leadership programs, conflict transformation programs, cooperative games/peaceful playground programs and appreciative parenting/families workshops. Email: info@taosinstitute.net

Jen Hetzel Silbert, MSOD, Principal of Innovation Partners International (www.innovationpartners.com), Charter Co-owner of Appreciative Inquiry Consulting LLC (www.aiconsulting.org), and an Associate of the Taos Institute is an experienced consultant, trainer, facilitator, and author supporting public, private, and social profit sector organizations in the US and around the world. Jen specializes in teaching and applying Appreciative Inquiry to systemic change, with particular focus on strategic planning, process  innovation, community development, change leadership, organization design, and family development. Her clients include the Rhode Island Department of Education, Sprint-Nextel, YMCA, the United Nations, the US Agency for International Development, the American Red Cross, and various social profit and youth-centered community groups, to include the Volunteer Center of RI (www.vcri.org) and Social Venture Partners of RI (www.svpri.org). Jen is based in South County, RI, where she lives with her husband, Tony, and two daughters, Brianna and Jocelyn. Email: jen@innovationpartners.com

Ada Jo Mann, Principal and President of Innovation Partners International (www.innovationpartners.com), has 35 years of experience collaborating with clients on people-centered approaches to strategic planning; program development and evaluation; inter-organizational partnerships; team building, and training. Through her work both in the US and abroad Ada Jo has increased the managerial capacities of a broad range of institutions including government agencies, bilateral and multilateral development organizations, non-profits and community groups. As Director of the GEM Initiative, she was a pioneer in the field of Appreciative Inquiry in the international development and social change arena and Founder and former Managing Co-Owner of Appreciative Inquiry Consulting, LLC (www.aiconsulting.org). Ada Jo is an Associate of the Taos Institute and is based in Washington, DC. Email: adajo@innovationpartners.com

Diana Whitney, Ph.D. President, Corporation for Positive Change (www.positivechange.org), Founder Emeritus of the Taos Institute (www.taosinstitute.net), and Distinguished Consulting Faculty at Saybrook Graduate School and Research Institute is an internationally recognized consultant, inspirational keynote speaker and executive coach who has authored and edited over 12 books on Appreciative Inquiry and Positive Change. She is a recipient of the ODN's Award for Contribution to the Field  for her writing and publications. Diana's consulting with businesses, NGOs, interfaith and educational organizations focuses on the application of Appreciative Inquiry for large scale transformation, strategic planning and leadership development. Her many and varied clients include Verizon, British Airways, Good Shepherd PMNA, and Unity. Her work with GTE won the ASTD Award for Best Culture Change. She is a visionary thought leader, a fellow of the World Business Academy, and on the faculty of Omega Institute, IMS and the NRC Picker Patient Centered Care Institute. She lives in Chapel Hill, NC. Email: diana@positivechange.org.

SHARE YOUR EXPERIENCES
AND STORIES WITH US

We invite you to share your experiences related to the ideas, questions and activities in this book. We would love to hear from you.

We want to know how the questions are working for you.

What new questions have you discovered that get great conversation going in your family and relationships?

What stories can you share about the power of the positive question?

What stories can you share about the transformational power of noticing and building upon the strengths, gifts and blessings of those we love?

Please take a few minutes and email us with your stories, reactions, observations, and affirmations.

Email: positivefamilies@windstream.net

APPRECIATIVE FAMILIES AND
APPRECIATIVE PARENTING WORKSHOPS

If you are interested in sponsoring or hosting a workshop on *Appreciative Families* or *Appreciative Parenting* in your area, contact us for more information. These workshops are a great opportunity to introduce the ideas and practices in this book to families and parents in schools, community centers, churches, synagogues, day care centers and health centers. We are happy to explore the possibilities with you.

Email: positivefamilies@windstream.net